THANKS FOR
YOUR HELP!
Ji [signature]

Best wishes
Edward F Rensslade [signature]

Thank you for a
great job!

[signature]

T U C S O N

HIGH DESERT HARMONY

TUCSON

HIGH DESERT HARMONY

INTRODUCTION BY THE RONSTADT FAMILY
ART DIRECTION BY GEOFFREY ELLIS

SPONSORED BY THE GREATER TUCSON ECONOMIC COUNCIL

URBAN TAPESTRY SERIES

TOWERY
PUBLISHING, INC.

CONTENTS

Library of Congress Cataloging-in-Publication data may be found on page 288.

8

Just as whole river systems can often be traced back to a single stream, the history of our family in Tucson can be traced to a single individual. The Ronstadt family first arrived here on April 23, 1882, in the person of Federico José María Ronstadt, known to all as Fred, a 14-year-old wagon shop apprentice.

Fred's legacy lies not merely with the successful business that he built here, or in the music that he loved and handed down to us, but also in his spirit of commitment to the community, a force that has driven numerous members of our family to become active participants in Tucson's civic life.

No better summary of Fred's love for Tucson and his new country can be found than in a message he once delivered to his employees. At the time, he was 81, nearing the end of his active career. Rereading his words, it is obvious that he wanted to pass on the awareness that living here is not merely a gift, but a blessing.

His words have not been forgotten: "We still know that no other country in the world can compare with ours. I say this not only because I know it, as every other American, but because of the gratitude I feel for the liberty and protection that I have enjoyed here for 67 years under the flag. I wonder how many of us fully appreciate the wonderful privilege of being a citizen of the United States?"

The Ronstadt family, from Fred's generation to the present, has continued to show its deep appreciation for these privileges through a long tradition of community service. ☞

© GILL KENNY

Joined by his brother, José María "Pepe" Ronstadt, who served as the postmaster of Tucson under Woodrow Wilson's presidency, Fred served on the Pima County Board of Supervisors. Addressing the issues of his time, he supported political candidates who were opposed to gambling and to allowing women in saloons. Fred's siblings and descendants have continued serving the public in various capacities over the years, as business and civic leaders, ranchers, and scoutmasters, and in other positions that have led to the continued success of our community. His grandsons once served the city as chief of police and director of parks and recreation while, currently, his great-grandson serves as a member of the Tucson City Council.

Throughout this rich family history runs the inspiration of Fred Ronstadt, whose example has served all of us well. His own story—which was captured in a memoir titled *Borderman*—is a fascinating one, revealing much about himself and his offspring, not to mention the history and development of modern-day Tucson.

After spending his boyhood in Sonora, Fred Ronstadt had reached an age where his parents needed to make a decision on his future. His father (whose name was Frederick), had planned to send his son either to Philadelphia to learn the shipbuilding trade or to Mexico City to a preparatory school for the military college. Mexican President Benito Pablo Juárez had granted a scholarship to the school for one of Frederick's sons.

But Fred's mother, Margarita Redondo, opposed the idea of military school and wanted her son to be near family. In Tucson, María Jesús Vásquez Dalton, Margarita's cousin, was

married to Winnall Dalton, co-owner of Dalton-Vásquez Carriage and Wagon Shop. The Ronstadt family reached a compromise, and young Fred was apprenticed to learn the wagon trade.

The next few years were devoted to learning the different aspects of the wagon and carriage business. Then, Fred left the wagon shop to work as a locomotive blacksmith and, in 1887, opened his own business. Over the course of the late 1800s and the first half of the 20th century, he built the F. Ronstadt Company into a thriving, diversified transportation, hardware, and machinery enterprise. As the transportation needs of Tucson changed over those years, so did the company's products and services.

While the F. Ronstadt Company had many locations, it always stayed downtown. As a matter of fact, one day, after Fred had moved his store to Camp Street, a gentleman arriving from New York City told him that all cities had a street named Broadway, but that he had not noticed one in Tucson. The visitor asked Fred if he would put up a sign reading Broadway on the side of his shop, which he did, and this is how Broadway Boulevard was named.

Tucson has long been at the crossroads of history, a history largely centered on the downtown area and revolving around one major local geographical attribute—the Santa Cruz River. And although the Ronstadts are considered one of modern Tucson's pioneer families, we have only been here for a small portion of its past, for the history of our community truly began thousands of years ago. ☞

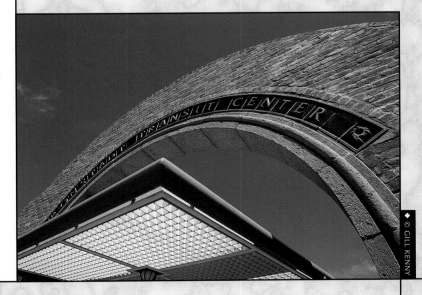

W hat makes a community unique? In the case of Tucson, rich history, diverse culture, and Old World tradition set our city apart from all others. We have a history that recognizes our valley as an outpost of Spanish, Mexican, and U.S. jurisdiction located in the midst of a long-settled Native American community. Our culture has been touched by the native population, as well as by all those who have traveled to and through the area. And we have centuries-old traditions that have been passed from parent to child in the longest continuously inhabited region in the United States.

Ours is the story of a community that for centuries has been the place to meet, trade, exchange ideas, enjoy festivals, and live in the wild, wild west. It is the story of a valley where the flags of the Tohono O'odham Nation, New Spain, Mexico, the Confederacy, the State of Arizona, and the United States all have flown.

In fact, we are the oldest community—and the oldest downtown—in the Northern Hemisphere. Settlement along the Santa Cruz River, near the foot of Sentinel Peak, has been continuous for 10,000 years. Native Americans, Spaniards, Mexicans, Chinese, Jews, Anglos, and African-Americans all have come to Tucson to live, work, and raise families. Each has brought distinctive traditions that through the years have come together into a unique spirit of Tucson—an indescribable, irreplaceable feeling one gets when surrounded by clear, starlit skies; majestic mountains; and the beautiful Sonoran Desert.

Some 10,000 years ago, during the Archaic period, inhabitants of the region hunted small game and harvested food along the Santa Cruz. Around A.D. 100, a new people,

© RICHARD CUMMINS / PHOTOPHILE

the Hohokams, began to cultivate maize on the fertile lands adjacent to the river. They developed trade routes extending into Mexico, California, and other areas in the west. The O'odham tribe, which succeeded the Hohokams, carried on the tradition of agriculture and trade, expanding irrigation canals from the Santa Cruz to enhance their use of the region's farmland.

Gradually, Europeans began making their way into the area. Spanish explorers Fray Marcos de Niza and Francisco Váquez de Coronado, leading expeditions from Mexico City just prior to 1540, made initial contact with the area's Native Americans. By 1600, Tucson had become part of the north-west frontier of New Spain.

Around 1690, Italian Jesuit missionary Father Eusebio Francisco Kino arrived in the area. Kino introduced a new religion, Spanish culture, new crops, and domesticated animals to the Tucson region—an entirely new way of life in an area the Spanish called Pimería Alta. Kino was one of many who, during the 18th century, established a series of Jesuit missions within Sonora, including the San Xavier Mission south of Tucson.

After the Jesuits were expelled by the Spanish Bourbon monarchy, a Franciscan influence began to take hold in the valley. Around 1770, Father Francisco Garces and Captain Juan Bautista de Anza, as a reaction to the possibility of Apache raids, arrived to supervise the construction of fortifi-cations at the San Agustín del Tucsón Mission near the base of Sentinel Peak. By 1800, a new chapel and a two-story *convento* complex were completed there. Today, the City of Tucson is working to forge a private/public partnership to

Mexican government in an effort to acquire the land as part of the United States. As a result of what became known as the Gadsden Purchase in December 1853, Tucson was forever removed as a political subdivision of Mexico.

By 1867, Tucson had become the capital of the Arizona Territory, a status it held for a decade. As further proof of the city's importance, in 1880, the Southern Pacific Railroad drove a silver spike into downtown, signifying the arrival of railroad transportation from California. Just one year later, the southern portion of the transcontinental railroad was completed, forever changing the face of Tucson. And while this new era in the history of Tucson arrived on two metal rails, a new era for the Ronstadt family—in the person of Fred Ronstadt—arrived here by way of a simple horse and wagon.

In the years following his arrival here, Fred and his progeny spent much of their time enjoying entertainment on Sunday afternoons in the Presidio and La Placita. Back in 1889, Fred started the first organized music group in Tucson— the Club Filarmónico Tucsonese—that provided much of the musical entertainment in the downtown community. The group practiced at the Elysian Grove until the city built a bandstand in La Placita Park.

Downtown was *the* place to be during most of that era. Generations of Ronstadts remember the equally vibrant downtown of the 1930s and 1940s, when people filled the streets to shop, transact business, or attend entertainment events. Saturday mornings were spent at the Fox Theater, watching cartoons and the weekly Flash Gordon episodes, or on trips to the downtown YMCA.

La Placita Village
110

8

Even today, with all of its regional wonders, Tucson's future as a world-class community revolves around the same place: our downtown. Its rich and colorful past is the palette from which our community is painting a picture for a bright tomorrow.

The physical remnants of past civilizations residing below our feet provide a solid foundation for the many cultures still reflected in the people of our community. Pieces of the original wall that surrounded the Spanish Presidio are being uncovered in ongoing archaeological digs throughout the area, known today as El Presidio. The largest piece of this fortress has been preserved for use in reconstruction of the Presidio as an interpretive cultural museum. There are building remnants of three different civilizations underneath this ground.

Many of Tucson's significant fine and performing arts venues are located downtown. The Temple of Music and Art, constructed in 1927 and restored in 1990, is home to the Arizona Theatre Company. The Leo Rich Theater and the Tucson Convention Center Arena and Music Hall are home to concerts, sporting events, the Tucson Symphony Orchestra, the Arizona Opera, the University of Arizona Icecats hockey program, and the International Mariachi Conference. The Tucson Museum of Art and Historic Block, located in El Presidio, encompasses some of the homes built by Tucson's early prominent citizens, as well as Tucson's oldest home, La Casa Cordova. The museum features permanent collections of pre-Columbian, Hispanic, western, and Asian art. Downtown is also home to the main branch of Tucson's public library, as well as the Tucson Children's Museum, which is located in the former Carnegie Library. ☞

Congress Street, once Tucson's "hip strip," is reemerging as the center of community entertainment. Vintage neon signs are being restored to adorn remodeled, early-20th-century storefronts. Nightclubs, restaurants, and niche retail stores offer residents and visitors a place to see and be seen. Two Roaring Twenties-era theaters, positioned much like bookends at opposite ends of Congress, are being renovated. The Fox Theatre, built in 1929 for cinema at the end of the silent-film period, features a southwestern art deco style that makes it perhaps the most architecturally significant theater in the state of Arizona. The Rialto Theatre was built in 1919 and was famous for its 1930s post-Prohibition entertainment, which included performances by Ginger Rogers. Entertainment at the Rialto delighted the likes of the notorious gangster John Dillinger, captured downtown in 1934 as a consequence of a fire at the Hotel Congress. These wonderful facilities fell into disrepair in the 1970s, but through the work of foundations, are being returned to their former grandeur.

New museums and cultural projects will play to our region's strengths: our fabulous and diverse southwestern history and culture; our proximity to Mexico and our cultural and economic ties to our growing neighbor to the south; and our leadership in astronomy and other natural sciences. The *convento*, which housed Spanish missionaries and is considered to be Tucson's birthplace, will be re-created and preserved as a cultural park at its original location at the base of Sentinel Peak. These cultural facilities will serve as wonderful amenities for Tucson residents, as well as outstanding destinations for tourists and conventioneers.

Several historic downtown buildings not only stand as

landmarks to Tucson's past, but also continue to play a part in the fabric of our community. The Charles O. Brown House is one of Tucson's oldest homes, and is now the home of El Centro Cultural de las Americas. St. Augustine Cathedral is not only a beautiful attraction, but remains an important place of worship. And for all of the history associated with the stylish Hotel Congress, it remains a vital part of the city's nightlife.

Tucson's downtown is surrounded by historic neighborhoods that trace their history from its roots as a dusty frontier town, continuing to the territorial days when the Old Pueblo (the city's longtime nickname) began to bustle as a railroad hub, and through the early 20th century, when Tucson began to mature as a modern city. Downtown's barrios, still home to descendants of early settlers, are characterized by the flat-roofed Sonoran houses set right up to the street.

The arrival of the Union Pacific Railroad in 1880 signaled the end of the region's isolation from the eastern part of the country, and became a catalyst for the social, economic, and architectural transformation of Tucson. The city's architecture began to incorporate Victorian design into Sonoran building forms. Later, the California bungalow style became popular.

The Armory Park and Iron Horse neighborhoods sprang up around the depot and its rail yards. The existing depot, built in 1907 on a site near Tombstone where Wyatt Earp shot a bandit who had escaped the law's reach, still provides vivid memories for Tucsonans who boarded the train there to serve our nation in World War II. The historic train depot is now the home of Amtrak and is being redeveloped for

modern-day commercial uses. Along with the nearby Ronstadt Transit Center—built in 1991 to commemorate the location of Fred's last store—the depot will provide the focal point of a multimodal transportation center into and out of the downtown.

The Tucson community has chosen to maintain downtown as its city center. Once the seat of Arizona's territorial legislature, downtown Tucson is home to local and regional government, as well as hundreds of businesses. More than 20,000 people work there every day, with another 3,000 visiting. There are currently more than 1 million square feet of office space downtown, and about 500,000 square feet of retail space.

As we move into the 21st century, Tucson will take on a greater leadership role as a focal point for trade with Latin America, as a center for excellence in optics and astronomy, and as a pioneer in solar technology and environmental preservation. Many of these activities will be carried out in our city center, with the same dedication and persistence that Fred Ronstadt bequeathed to us when he arrived here more than a century ago. The region will continue to look to downtown as the seat of government, and as a center of art, culture, and entertainment. And out-of-town visitors will find downtown to be a delightful place that tells Tucson's story like no other place can. After all, downtown Tucson is where it has been happening in this beautiful valley for more than 10,000 years. ◊

▲ © JAMES RANDKLEV

WHILE THE POTENTIAL OF TUCSON MAY be boundless, some things do have their limits. Two-term Mayor George Miller (LEFT) imposed his own when he decided not to seek election to another term in November 1999. And it's the mountains that form the geographic edges of the city itself— the Santa Catalinas on the north, the Tucson Mountains to the west, the Rincons on the east, and the Santa Ritas down south.

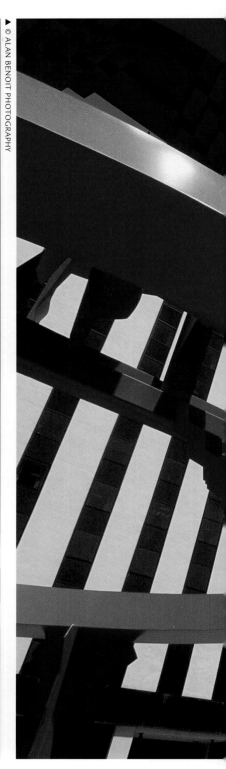

The old PIMA COUNTY COURTHOUSE on Church Street is one of downtown's best-known landmarks (OPPOSITE). Designed by local architect Roy Place and built in 1928, it features a 32-foot-diameter dome covered with brightly colored, glazed tile. With a more modern twist, artist David Black's towering metal sculpture, *Sonora*, welcomes students of all ages to the Tucson-Pima Public Library (ABOVE).

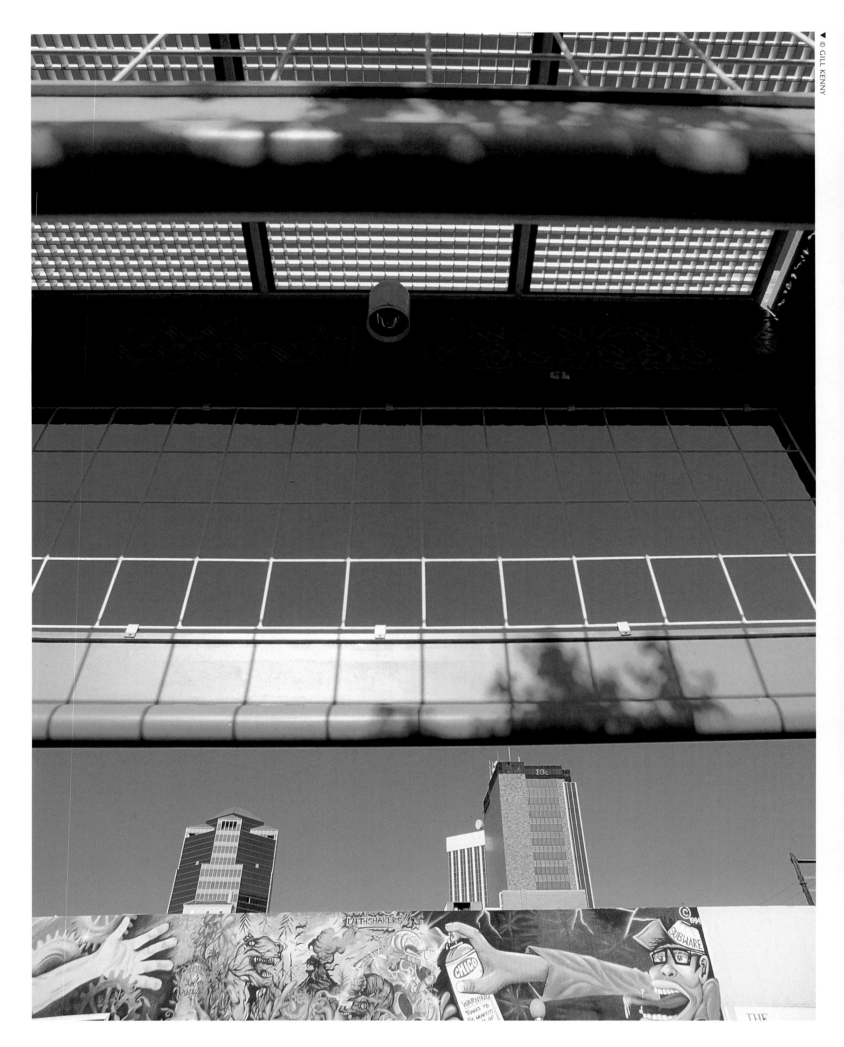

FROM THE CREATIVELY DECORATED Greyhound-Trailways bus terminal (OPPOSITE) to the shiny Norwest Tower (LEFT), the face of downtown Tucson has changed throughout the years. On Church Avenue, however, there is one monument that has withstood the test of time: a one-ton clock brought to town in the 1930s by Elmer Present, a jeweler who used it to advertise his business.

THE GOVERNMENT AND BUSINESS offices that make up downtown reflect different eras and different design philosophies, from the tiered, 23-story Norwest Tower (TOP) to the State of Arizona's office complex (BOTTOM). Built in stages, beginning in 1960 when the City Council chambers opened, City Hall today has far outgrown the 500 or so employees who work there (OPPOSITE). Plans are under way for a new facility.

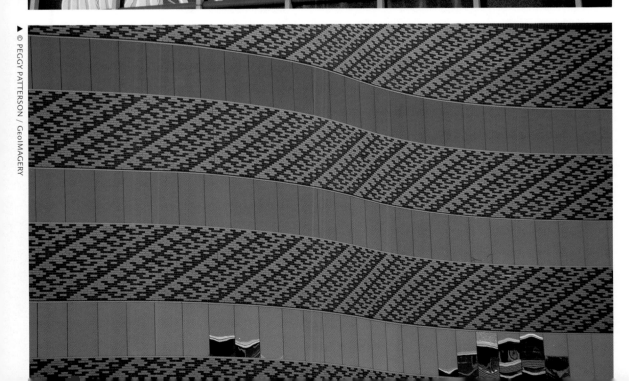

ADULT DENTAL CARE
WHERE ART MEETS SCIENCE
ROGER B. ANDERSON, DMD, FAGD

E VEN THE METROPOLITAN TUCSON Convention & Visitors Bureau can't claim that you'll run into smiling faces everywhere you go in the city, but you never know where you'll encounter a terra-cotta grin or a business sign that greets you like an old friend. After all, you have to expect a certain amount of whimsy from a town where one street alone— Tanque Verde Road—features a life-size *Tyrannosaurus rex*, a stagecoach on top of a rock, and a kid-sized, fully functional train.

Tucson Museum of Art

THE ART OF LIVING: LOCATED ON THE site of Tucson's Spanish Presidio, the Tucson Museum of Art (ABOVE) plays host to a wide variety of works from pre-Columbian to contemporary.

Not to be outdone, Truly Nolen Exterminating, Inc. has become locally renowned for the floral mural adorning its headquarters on East Speedway Boulevard (OPPOSITE).

TUCSON'S VARIETY OF MUSEUMS, galleries, and performance halls promises a venue for any artist. Woman-Kraft Castle Art Center (OPPOSITE) is home to exhibits and classes empha- sizing women artists, while some of the finest Native American artists and craftspeople from around the region find a forum at the Arizona State Museum (TOP). The Temple of Music and Art (BOTTOM) hosts the Arizona Theatre Company, which performs a full range of plays from September through May each year.

TUCSON

Perhaps no Arizona artist is better known than Ettore "Ted" De Grazia (1909-1982), a painter-sculptor-ceramist who specialized in bold, simple, colorful scenes of the Southwest. His depictions of Native American children, drawn with round faces and virtually sans features, have become almost a symbol of this region. His widow, Marion (OPPOSITE RIGHT), still works at the renowned De Grazia Gallery in the Sun (OPPOSITE LEFT AND ABOVE).

ARTISTS LYNN TABER (THIS PAGE) AND Michael Stack (OPPOSITE) are drawn to depicting the dramatic beauty of Southwest skies, which natives will attest are like nowhere else in the world—especially during the summer rainy season.

TUCSON BOASTS SEVERAL INSTITUTIONS of higher learning, including the University of Arizona (OPPOSITE) and Pima Community College. In addition to private schools of every size and curriculum, the city also maintains a multidistrict public school system that has nurtured the talents of people as diverse as astronaut Frank Borman and science fiction writer Ray Bradbury.

THE UNIVERSITY OF ARIZONA'S PACIFIC-10 Conference sports program has racked up national championships in basketball and softball, and nurtured the careers of pro athletes such as NBA stars Sean Elliott and Steve Kerr. The community is enthusiastic about showing its support for the Wildcats, and symptoms of Wildcat fever include showing up at games to see players like quarterback Ortege Jenkins (OPPOSITE, BOTTOM LEFT).

THE CITY IS ALWAYS READY TO PARTY, and two of the biggest annual fun-and-games blowouts are the University of Arizona's Spring Fling (OPPOSITE) and the 77-year-old Pima County Fair, whose midway attractions, concerts, and livestock shows bring about 380,000 visitors to the fairgrounds.

THE RICH HISTORY AND DESERT GEOG-
raphy of Tucson provide inspiration

carefully gloved—hands. At Santa Cruz
River Park, a mosaic speaks to the role

the Santa
cruz was
the river of
Life to the
people who
first Lived

I F YOU WANT THE BEST VIEW OF A SUNSET, natives will instruct you to head west— out Speedway Boulevard through Gates Pass to Saguaro National Park, where the huge native cacti provide a thrilling accent to the bright, white glow of the moon; the spreading crimson and gold of the sun's descent; or the electricity of a summer storm (PAGES 64-69).

▲ © HEATHER GRAVNING

I N TUCSON, SUMMER STORMS OFTEN materialize from cloudless skies and are fantastic sound-and-light shows, punctuated with lightning of Frankensteinian proportions.

TUCSON

FROM THE DRY, ROLLING DESERT TO THE tall, wooded peaks of the surrounding mountains, Tucson runs the gamut of terrain. It is said—with more than a grain of truth—that in December, Tucsonans can take a dip in the pool, then jump in the car and drive for an hour up to Ski Valley on Mount Lemmon in the Santa Catalinas, where they can strap on their skis and hit the slopes.

S OME 115 MILES EAST OF TUCSON LIES rugged Chiricahua National Monument, a scenic and serene site in the midst of the Chiricahua Mountains.

Once home to the Apaches, the area now contains popular hiking trails that take visitors through a dwarf forest and up to monoliths of volcanic formations—such as Big Balanced Rock (ABOVE)—carved from erosion wrought by wind and rain.

N O ONE WILL EVER MISTAKE THE PEAKS
around Tucson for the Himalayas,
but there are many lofty stretches that
can challenge even experienced rock
climbers.

TUCSONANS ARE CRAZY ABOUT ROCKS— and not just the ones that occur naturally. If they're not climbing the real thing at Windy Point on Mount Lemmon (OPPOSITE), they're putting a ball through one at Magic Carpet Golf and Games (ABOVE).

THEY GROW 'EM BIG IN TUCSON. A giant statue of Paul Bunyan guards the entrance to an auto supply store on North Stone Avenue (OPPOSITE). Around Christmastime, he's been known to sport a red stocking cap and hold a huge candy cane. The oversized creatures at Magic Carpet Golf and Games have been delighting the city's kids and grown-ups alike for many years.

W HOA THERE, PARDNER. WESTERN
pride abounds in Tucson. From
the rodeo arena and the racetrack to
painted brick walls, riders are known to
be on the lookout for a quick buck
(PAGES 84-87).

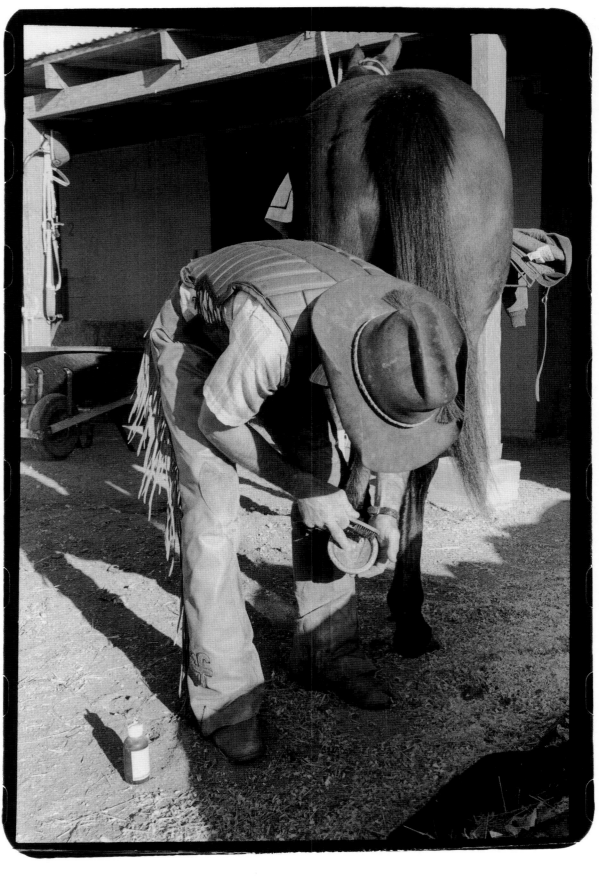

Country singer Willie Nelson advises, "Mamas, don't let your babies grow up to be cowboys." Once suggesting a rough and wild lifestyle as much as a line of employment, today the designation "cowboy" is a badge worn with pride and a symbol of a vanishing way of life.

ALL OVER THE SOUTHWEST, VISITORS will find reminders of the highly romanticized, dramatic life of the settlers of the frontier. Were the border bandits liberators or outlaws? The authenticity of these depictions is open to debate, and the politics can be difficult to untangle, but the popularity of the images brings in visitors from all over the world.

OLD TUCSON STUDIOS ON KINNEY ROAD was initially built for the 1940 film *Arizona*, starring William Holden and Jean Arthur. A long list of productions fol-lowed, and in time, it developed into a theme park. Not a ghost studio yet, por-tions of films, TV shows, music videos, and commercials are still shot there.

WESTERN TRADITIONS LIVE ON IN Tucson. In the heart of downtown, a wishing shrine for failed lovers, known as *El Tiradito* (TOP), has been the repository for devotional candles for more than 100 years. Celebrations and epitaphs honoring the dead are also part of the area's unique culture. A beautiful stained glass angel watches over one cemetery, and flowers decorate the graves of loved ones in honor of *El Día de los Muertos*—"the day of the dead" (MIDDLE). In the once-prosperous mining town of Tombstone, visitors flock to the graves of western outlaws, where the markers hold epitaphs rich in detail and humor (BOTTOM).

DUE TO ITS EARLY HISTORY OF SPANISH Catholicism, the Tucson area supports more than three dozen Catholic churches—yielding a proliferation of religious icons available at shops, swap meets, and even the occasional yard sale.

Carlo Giantomassi (above) and Donatella Zari, a husband-and-wife team from Rome, put together an international group of conservation experts for a $2 million interior restoration of Mission San Xavier del Bac. Located on the Tohono O'odham Nation's San Xavier Reservation, the site is a more-than-200-year-old, fully operational Catholic church. Over the years, dust and candle soot had darkened its wall paintings and statues, but today, the results of years of the restoration effort are spectacular (pages 102 and 103).

S TUNNING IN ANY LIGHT, THE MEXICAN baroque facade and towers of St. Augustine Cathedral (ABOVE), completed in 1928, feature a historic cast stone depiction of the history of faith in the Southwest. Known as the White Dove of the Desert due to its shimmering appearance, Mission San Xavier del Bac (OPPOSITE)—another Mexican baroque masterpiece—was completed in 1797.

M ODELED AFTER THE CATHEDRAL OF Querétaro, St. Augustine Cathedral is named after Tucson's patron saint. Its interior is filled with the religious statuary of the Catholic faith.

Tumacacori National Historical Park, near the Arizona-Mexico border, occupies an area believed to be one of the first settled by Europeans venturing into what is now the United States. Founded in the late 1600s by Father Eusebio Francisco Kino as one of 24 missions, the site today features a colonial Spanish-style church built in the 1800s and a visitor center, itself a historic building completed in 1937.

THE USE OF SUNBAKED MUD BRICKS, A material known as adobe, proved to be an excellent way of dealing with the Southwest's hot, desert temperatures as more and more settlers moved into the area. Today, adobe structures remain a permanent part of Tucson's landscape.

BOLD COLORS SAY "RESTORATION" FOR these historic homes in Tucson's Barrio Viejo. Throughout the barrio, former residences have been converted for use as business offices, shops, restaurants, and bed-and-breakfast inns.

LA PLACITA VILLAGE, A RECENTLY REFUR-
bished office complex, is just one
of Tucson's attempts to lure businesses
and people back into the city's struggling downtown. Its bright colors reflect
elements of the community's Mexican
heritage, and are great companion
pieces to the murals that enliven
downtown walls.

A WALKING TOUR OF BARRIO VIEJO IS mandatory for anyone who wants to understand Tucson's roots. Within a few square blocks, visitors can see everything from humble adobe dwell- ings to massive mansions that housed the city's movers and shakers. The Manning House (OPPOSITE, TOP LEFT) was built in 1907 by former Mayor Levi Howell Manning. It is slightly predated by the Spanish-mission-style Steinfeld House (OPPOSITE, TOP RIGHT), once belonging to one of the most powerful merchants in Tucson. And the Owl's Club Mansion (OPPOSITE, BOTTOM RIGHT) is distinctive for its Pepto-Bismol color and unusual exterior accoutrements.

TODAY, ALTHOUGH COMMUNAL AQUATIC facilities thrive, there are some 40,000 in-ground pools at private homes in Pima County. The residents of Tucson long ago equated a swimming pool with summer survival.

F OR THOSE SEEKING TOTAL RELAXATION with a twist of history, the Arizona Inn (OPPOSITE) is a reminder of the old days when Tucson was primarily a resort area. Built in 1930 by the state's first congresswoman, Isabella Greenway, the inn's 14 acres are as popular today as ever. More recent, but no less impressive, the Sheraton El Conquistador Resort & Country Club (ABOVE) offers a huge pool with a swim-up bar, golf courses with incredible views, and restaurants like the western-themed Last Territory Steakhouse and Music Hall.

WATER ACTIVITY IN TUCSON ISN'T JUST for fun—it's also for games. Olympic gold and silver medalist Crissy Ahmann and her son Alex Leighton (BOTTOM) might be relaxing now, but she came out of retirement in 1996 in an unsuccessful bid to become the first mom ever to make the U.S. Olympic swimming team.

Tucsonans have reached for the stars in many ways. At the University of Arizona's Steward Observatory Mirror Laboratory (OPPOSITE), advances in celestial viewing—such as a 6.5-meter honeycomb mirror—have kept the facility at the top of the telescope field. In southern Arizona, the Fred L. Whipple Observatory on Mount Hopkins (ABOVE) is home to a 10-meter gamma ray reflector, designed for the capture of light particles striking the upper atmosphere.

Kitt Peak National Observatory, located southwest of Tucson in the Quinlan Mountains, has the largest selection of optical telescopes in the world. One of the most impressive instruments on the mountain is the McMath-Pierce solar telescope, the world's largest and most sophisticated scope designed for studying the sun.

Built in 1991 just north of Tucson, the 3.15-acre Biosphere 2 (PAGES 128-129) was initially a human terrarium, designed as a prototype for space colonization efforts. Today, operated by Columbia University, the almost $200 million facility hosts a number of earth science studies and experiments in the seven wilderness ecosystems under its dome.

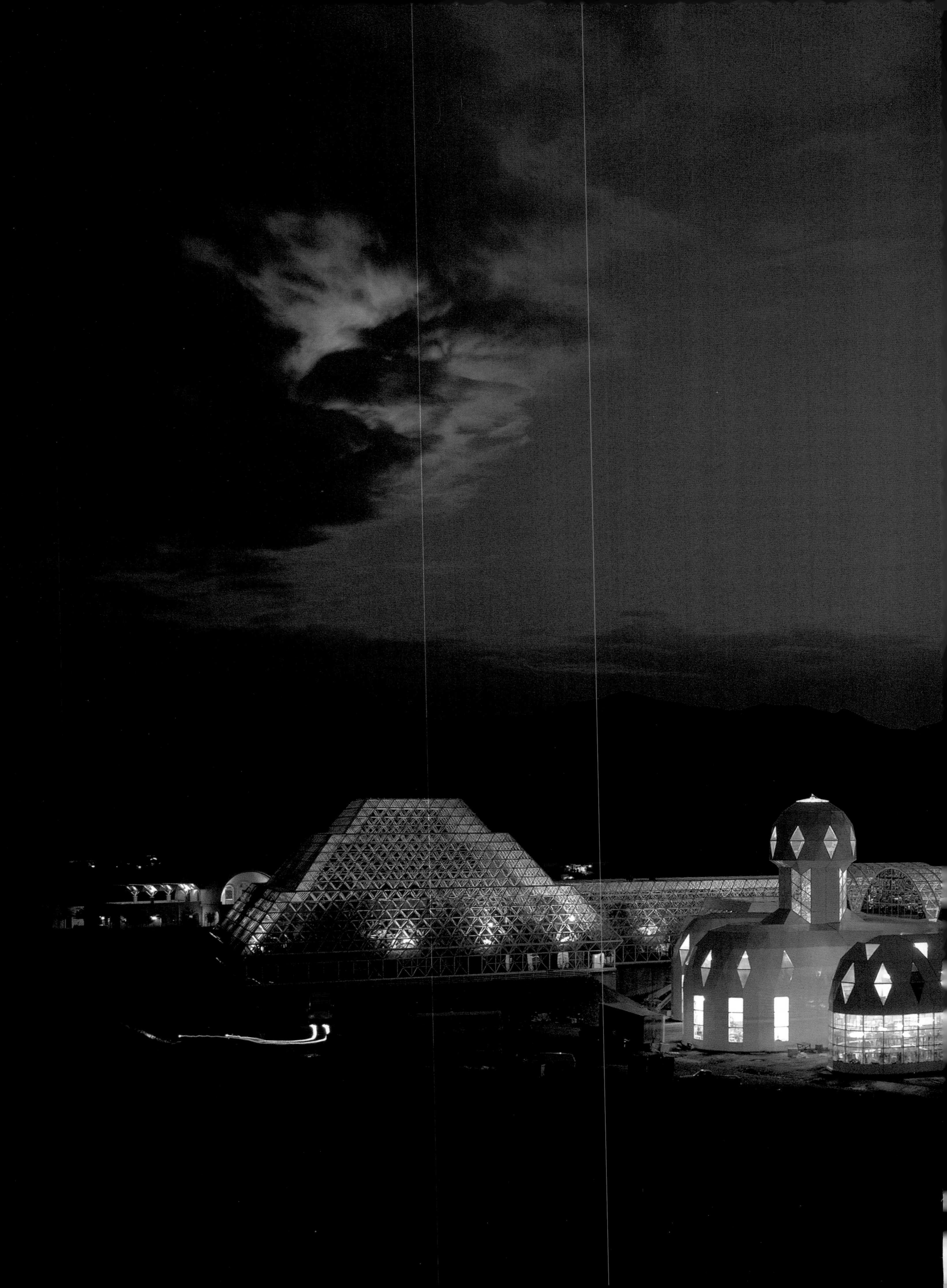

◆ © GILL KENNY

T HE LARGEST INTERCONTINENTAL BALLIS-
tic missile (ICBM) ever made by the
United States, the Titan II was only to
be fired in response to a Soviet first

strike during the Cold War. Today, the
Titan Missile Museum allows visitors
an up close and personal look at the
ICBM site near Green Valley, where

the 103-foot-tall missile, control room,
and sleeping quarters for the crew are
on display.

WHETHER FLYING HIGH ABOVE PICACHO Peak or soaring through an afternoon of exercise, Tucsonans enjoy spreading their wings.

MORE THAN 200 MILITARY, COMMERcial, and private aircraft are on permanent display at the Pima Air & Space Museum (ABOVE), including the SR-71 Blackbird, the world's highest-flying and fastest aircraft. Across the street at Davis-Monthan Air Force Base's Aerospace Maintenance and Regeneration Center—otherwise known as the Boneyard—some well-used aircraft come to their final resting place, while others are recycled or sold (OPPOSITE).

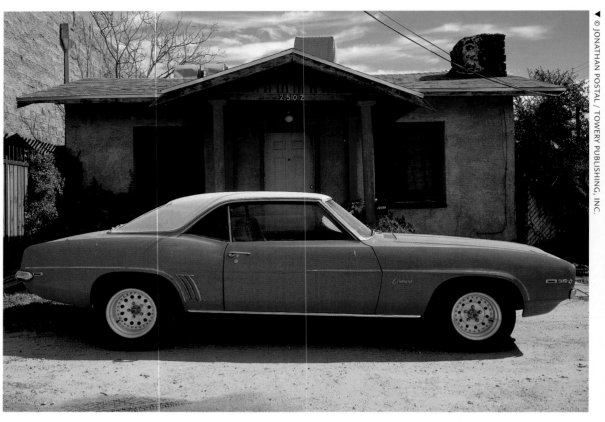

Tucson's love affair with racing dates back to the days when automobiles were little more than a curiosity, even luring racer Eddie Rickenbacker (BOTTOM) to town for an early heat at Steinfeld Track. More than three-quarters of a century later, Tucson Raceway Park and Southwestern International Raceway are the hot tickets for hot-rodders such as Brian Lopez.

FROM OLD TUCSON STUDIOS' CHILD-sized locomotive (OPPOSITE), to Fourth Avenue's Old Pueblo Trolley (ABOVE LEFT), Tucsonans love to ride the rails. For some, however, nothing's as groovy as wheelin' about on a good ol' bike.

ONE WRITER REFERRED TO TUCSON'S Miracle Mile as "a sea of trailer parks and cheap hotels." But beauty is clearly in the eye of the beholder (PAGES 140-143). The motel strip north of downtown is a haven for those into Americana, with names like Riviera and Flamingo attracting tourists yearning for kitsch.

S ITUATED IN THE HEART OF DOWNTOWN, the 40-room Hotel Congress looks about the same as it did in 1934 when the infamous John Dillinger gang reportedly rented rooms there. Built in 1919 for railroad passengers, the downtown spot now offers three establishments worthy of Tucson nightlife: the Cup Café, legendary for its desserts; the Tap Room, a neighborhood-bar-type hangout; and the Club Congress, a night-club that is definitely a little bit this and a little bit that.

M ORE THAN 50 YEARS AGO, THEIR parents were doing the lindy hop and the jitterbug at the Blue Moon on North Oracle Road; today, modern swing kids crowd the dance floor at the restored Rialto Theatre.

WHILE SOME TEENS MIGHT FIND A BIT of appeal in hanging around like a bunch of dummies, Gabriella Contreras (OPPOSITE) has had other ideas—and how. As a third grader, she founded Club BADDD (Be Alert—Don't Do Drugs); at 13, she was honored with a Prudential Spirit of Community Award as one of the nation's top 10 youth volunteers.

Tucson may have a reputation as a community of goat ropers with a few buttoned-down corporate types thrown in, but we still know how to walk on the wild side now and again, as demonstrated by dancer/actress Nikki Arizona (LEFT) and tattoo artist Tracy Ledbetter (OPPOSITE).

Tucson's musical heritage is deep and wide. Rock goddess LeeAnne Savage (OPPOSITE) and her band, Shockadelica, have obedient followers lined up 20 deep to see them in venues throughout southern Arizona. Jazz musicians such as Janice Jarrett (ABOVE) have developed a more relaxed—though no less fervent—fan base.

THE PLAY'S THE THING. CHILDREN'S theater is big in Tucson, and kids even perform as extras in productions by the Arizona Opera (OPPOSITE). Baritone Ben Sorenson (LEFT), in addition to his performances with the opera, teaches music at Pima Community College.

THE OLD WEST HAD ITS SHARE OF colorful characters, as does modern Tucson. Four local favorites are Maestro George Hanson, conductor of the Tucson Symphony Orchestra (RIGHT); rocker and San Jacinto Records President Rich Hopkins (LEFT); country singer/ songwriter Chuck Maultsby (OPPOSITE RIGHT); and *Tucson Weekly* columnist Jeff Smith (OPPOSITE LEFT).

MARCHING TO THEIR OWN BEATS, Tucson's musicians are a varied lot. In a remarkable accomplishment of longevity, Grammy-nominated flutist R. Carlos Nakai (OPPOSITE LEFT) recently issued his 27th recording. His fellow musicians, though perhaps less famous, nonetheless make a significant contribution to the sweet sounds of success.

A RAINBOW OF CULTURES COME TOGETHER to create the fabric of Tucson (PAGES 160-163). Influences from the area's Native American population mix well with the region's Spanish history, resulting in a whirling blanket of activity.

Decades-old traditions and cutting-edge gourmet food go hand in hand in Tucson. The Flores family (opposite) has been operating El Charro Cafe and serving time-honored recipes since the 1930s. Across town, Chef Janos Wilder (above) serves up wholly original variations on southwestern nouvelle cuisine.

P ATRIOTIC DISPLAYS ARE COMMONPLACE
in the community, where parades
are held for everything from Memorial
Day to Cinco de Mayo.

Tucson's citizens have made valuable contributions to their city—and beyond. Ned Norris Jr. (above) runs the Desert Diamond Casino on the Tohono O'odham Reservation, securing the future for his centuries-old tribe. During World War II, Betty Tucker (opposite) played in the All-American Girls Professional Baseball League, the basis for the movie *A League of Their Own*.

Though definitely not a retirement community, Tucson has a large number of retirees, split between natives and newcomers. Part of the attraction of the city is the active lifestyle, which includes everything from the competitive weight lifting familiar to former Mr. Arizona Johnny Gibson (ABOVE) to the tap dancing revues of the Hot Flashes (OPPOSITE).

THE CITY'S POLICE AND FIRE DEPART-
ments were both created back in
the days of the wild and woolly West,
when flames were as big a threat on
the frontier as bullets—a trend that
continues to this day.

B ACK IN THE OLD DAYS, CIRCA 1912, newsies helped spread the word about the goings-on in the community through the sale of the *Tucson Daily Citizen* (now the *Tucson Citizen*), the oldest continuously published newspaper in the state. But whatever hat you wear in modern Tucson, there's a job to be done in the region's booming economy.

176

I T'S BUSINESS AS USUAL FOR PROFESSIONALS in Tucson, some of whom take advantage of the city's temperate weather to relax outside downtown's Tucson-Pima County Public Library (BOTTOM RIGHT).

Tucson Heart Hospital

TUCSON HEART HOSPITAL (OPPOSITE), A $34 million complex dedicated to cardiology and cardiovascular services, is part of the new look of the city, which includes a variety of buildings—such as the Woods Memorial Branch Library (ABOVE)—that have recently received stylish face-lifts.

THE TUCSON CONVENTION CENTER, built where part of Barrio Viejo once stood, is host to a myriad of community events. The facility features a music hall, a small theater, an arena (known as the Madhouse on Main Street when the Icecats hockey team plays there), a galleria, and an exhibit hall.

T HE 80,000 ACRES OF SAGUARO NATIONAL
Park are arguably the most photographed, most visited acres in the
area, and it's impossible to understand
the lure of Tucson without seeing them
firsthand (PAGES 182-183).

D RIVING THROUGH THE TWISTING, narrow turns of Gates Pass, visitors and locals alike are reminded of two things: first, that the Sonoran Desert is a place of awesome sights, and, second, that the men and women who came to settle this rocky region on foot, on horseback, and in rickety stagecoaches were nothing short of fearless.

DISCOVERED IN 1974 AND OPENED to the public in 1999, Kartchner Caverns State Park qualifies as a living cave. Aided by a 99 percent humidity rate, the site's incredible multicolor formations continue to grow (PAGES 186-189).

WORKS BY ARTISTS MICHAEL STACK—
Evening Rain in a Desert Land
(ABOVE)—and Lynn Taber—*Midsummer
in Tucson* (OPPOSITE)—capture the beauty
of Tucson's skies and the high desert
harmony that makes this place unique.

96 KLPX
TUCSON ROCK-N-ROLL

1854 - 1975

EFORE THE UNIVERSITY OF ARIZONA WAS FOUNDED, BEFORE CITY HALL WAS BUILT, EVEN BEFORE ARIZONA WAS A STATE, THE U.S. POSTAL SERVICE WAS AN ESTABLISHED FIXTURE IN TUCSON. ONE OF THE FIRST INSTITUTIONS IN THE CITY, THE

postal service provided Arizona miners, ranchers, homesteaders, farmers, and missionaries with everything from paychecks to soap to clothing to food, and served as their main link with the rest of the world.

Nineteenth-century Tucson was full of challenges: ordinary men, intent on making extraordinary fortunes, drove picks deep into the mountainside of the area. In 1854, as a part of the Gadsden Purchase, mail started coming into the territory and the first post office was established.

Hiram Reed was appointed the first postmaster of the city once Arizona became a territory in 1863. During territorial days, it was treacherous to get mail delivered. Mail for California gold rush miners often was sent on boats around South America. Tucson's mail came by rail, and it was often easier to take a letter directly to the train station than to take it to the local post office.

INTO THE NEW MILLENNIUM

Today, the Tucson Post Office faces many different challenges, including the booming growth and seasonal changes in population. Each day, the post office in Tucson delivers to more than 500,000 mailboxes for the more than 1 million people in the area, including towns in the 857 and 856 ZIP codes—Green Valley, Douglas, Bisbee, and Nogales.

"Our state is one of the fastest growing in America right now," says Tucson Postmaster Alvaro A. Alvarez. "The challenge is to keep up with growth." The post office has long-range plans that predict which area of the city will experience population growth. Stations in Oro Valley and on Tucson's southwest side are among the newest post office facilities, and more facilities are planned for the northwest and east sides of town.

"We have a large forwarding operation," comments Alvarez, "as the many winter visitors, who come to Tucson to avoid the harsh winters in their home

EACH DAY, THE TUCSON POST OFFICE DELIVERS TO MORE THAN 500,000 MAILBOXES FOR THE MORE THAN 1 MILLION PEOPLE IN THE AREA (TOP AND BOTTOM).

states, return home in the spring. The winter visitors also bring with them more mail for us to deliver in our winter months."

The Tucson main post office also houses the plant and distribution center for the area. This is a three-tier, 24-hour operation that processes not only outgoing mail for the area but incoming mail for the city each day. This mail goes to postal stations early each morning for delivery to homes and businesses. The Plant and Distribution Center is ever changing as new equipment is installed to provide better, more efficient mail delivery.

MEETING CLIENTS' NEEDS

The post office also predicts what kind of services residents will require of a postal station. It must also deal with fluctuations in the number of its customers, brought on by the city's mild winters and blazing summers. Says Alvarez, "Seasonal residents live in several different parts of the city, and the postal service has cultivated long-term relationships with many of them."

Often, postal workers from other parts of the United States want to transfer to Tucson as well, which gives the post office a large pool of qualified personnel to choose from. "We have the ability to pick the best," says Alvarez. The Tucson post office also maintains friendships across the border, sending used postal equipment to Mexico.

By becoming more corporate in its operation, the post office has become better able to respond to the changing needs of consumers. One change has

been an increased awareness of the need to market stamps. For example, the post office helped educate people around the world about the Sonoran Desert in 1999, when it issued a special stamp depicting Tucson's flora and fauna, such as saguaro cacti and Gambel's quail. It was the first time a stamp was embedded in scenery—each stamp showed a different plant or

animal from a different part of the overall painting, instead of depicting a miniature version of the whole scene.

Today, the postal service is a part of every citizen's daily routine. The millions of pieces of mail sent and received every year are testament to the fact that after a century and a half, the Tucson Postal Service still delivers.

THE PLANT AND DISTRIBUTION CENTER IS EVER CHANGING AS NEW EQUIPMENT IS INSTALLED TO PROVIDE BETTER, MORE EFFICIENT MAIL DELIVERY.

THE POST OFFICE HAS LONG-RANGE PLANS, WHICH INCLUDE SERVING AREAS OF PREDICTED POPULATION GROWTH.

WO OF ARIZONA'S OLDEST PUBLICATIONS, *THE ARIZONA DAILY STAR* AND *TUCSON CITIZEN*, MAKE UP THE CORE OF TUCSON NEWSPAPERS, A PARTNERSHIP THAT STAYS YOUNG AT HEART BY KEEPING UP WITH TUCSON'S AMAZING GROWTH. ■ TUCSON'S

morning newspaper, the *Star*, and the afternoon newspaper, the *Citizen*, are linked by a joint operating agreement that provides a shared business agency, doing business as Tucson Newspapers (TNI). Though the two are separately owned and maintain separate editorial staffs, they share the services of the TNI staff and facilities, including the main building on South Park Avenue.

Though each newspaper is more than 120 years old, each stays current with state-of-the-art computers, software, processes, and printing equipment, and each is fully engaged in the Internet revolution with its own Web site.

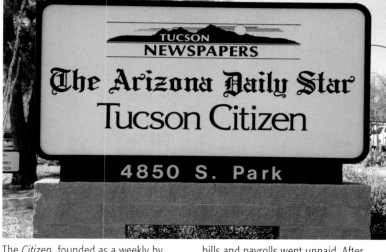

THE TUCSON CITIZEN

The oldest continuously published newspaper in the state, the *Tucson Citizen* has provided news and information to readers in southern Arizona since 1870.

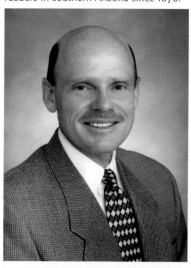

The *Citizen*, founded as a weekly by John Wasson and Richard Cunningham McCormick, went daily in 1879, and, except for a brief move to Florence, Arizona, soon after it was founded, it has been a part of Tucson since frontier days. McCormick, a Republican, financed the paper with the aim of publicizing his successful campaign to be elected a representative of the Arizona territory.

By February 1910, the newspaper was sold to Tucson Printing and Publishing Co., headed by James T. Williams. It was about that time that the *Citizen* began its evolution toward a more cosmopolitan newspaper, with more news, political cartoons, and feature stories illustrated by line drawings. The *Citizen* was successful until 1928, when Frank H. Hitchcock acquired controlling interest in the paper, but during the depression, ad sales and circulation plummeted, and

bills and payrolls went unpaid. After Hitchcock's death in 1936, the *Citizen* was sold to William A. Small.

In 1940, Small helped form a joint operating agency with the *Arizona Daily Star*, which resulted in the two papers combining their business and mechanical functions in a common building—the *Star*'s office on North Stone Avenue. The papers remained separate and competitive in news operations, while the new agency, then called Tucson Newspapers, Inc., handled advertising, circulation, and printing for both. The partnership continues to this day, surviving an antitrust challenge that led to the passage of the 1971 Newspaper Preservation Act.

As the circulation grew, so did the papers' location on Stone Avenue. The building doubled in size in the mid-1950s, and seven new press units were added. The papers grew still larger, and moved in 1973 into their current headquarters at Park Avenue and Irvington Road. The Small family sold the *Citizen* in 1976 to Gannett Co., Inc., the nation's largest newspaper group. C. Donald Hatfield is the present editor and publisher. Michael Limon is managing editor.

When the papers' joint operating agreement was renegotiated in 1989, the agency corporation was dissolved and a partnership was formed. The accounting, marketing, and personnel departments of the *Star* and *Citizen* were added to the agency, which was renamed TNI Partners.

CLOCKWISE FROM TOP:

THE ARIZONA DAILY STAR AND *TUCSON CITIZEN*, TWO OF ARIZONA'S OLDEST PUBLICATIONS, MAKE UP THE CORE OF TNI, A PARTNERSHIP THAT STAYS YOUNG AT HEART BY KEEPING UP WITH TUCSON'S AMAZING GROWTH.

THOUGH THE *STAR* AND *CITIZEN* ARE SEPARATELY OWNED AND MAINTAIN SEPARATE EDITORIAL STAFFS, THEY SHARE THE SERVICES OF THE TNI STAFF AND THE FACILITIES, INCLUDING THE PRODUCTION FACILITY ON SOUTH PARK AVENUE.

LARRY ALDRICH, PRESIDENT AND CEO OF TNI

Like the city of Tucson, the *Citizen* has changed greatly since its early days. But the paper's continuing commitment to the community is reflected in its slogan: The *Citizen* is Tucson.

THE ARIZONA DAILY STAR

A hand-operated press produced the first issues of the *Arizona Daily Star* in 1877. Today, the paper is a leader in communications technology, answering the changing information needs of its fast-growing community of more than 800,000 residents.

L.C. Hughes, a liberal Pennsylvania lawyer, started his newspaper—originally called the *Daily Bulletin*—in partnership with printer Charles H. Tully. Hughes and Tully couldn't muster enough early support for the *Daily Bulletin*, so it ceased publication after just 28 days. The paper was reborn as the *Tri-Weekly Star,* and later the *Weekly Star,* before resuming daily publication for good in 1879.

Hughes was aided in his venture by his wife, E. Josephine Brawley Hughes, an early champion of women's rights. Known as "the mother of Arizona," Josephine Hughes established the first Protestant church in Tucson. She eventually took over the *Star* as her husband shifted his attention to his other endeavors.

In 1907, the Hugheses sold the paper, and three years later, it fell into the hands of the Phelps-Dodge Copper Company, an early chain of Arizona newspapers, and E.E. Ellinwood, a copper company lawyer. Ellinwood installed his son Ralph as editor, putting him in partnership with

Business Manager William R. Mathews, who took over the *Star* after Ralph Ellinwood's death at age 37. Mathews went on to get an exclusive interview with exiled revolutionary Leon Trotsky, predict in print the bombing of Pearl Harbor, witness the Japanese surrender aboard the USS *Missouri*, and cover the Vietnam War.

Mathews also handpicked political candidates, shamed football teams into allowing African-Americans to play, and mounted a failed campaign for Congress. He saw the paper through a devastating fire and the Great Depression. In 1959, a researcher from Michigan State University said he couldn't find another person in America who had more influence over a

community's decision making than Mathews.

Citizen owner Small bought the *Star* from Mathews in 1965 and owned both papers for six years before selling the *Star* to the Pulitzer Publishing Company.

In 1971, Michael Pulitzer took over as editor and publisher of the *Star*. He named Stephen E. Auslander executive editor in 1986 and editor in 1991. Bobbie Jo Buel, who has worked as a reporter and editor, was appointed managing editor in 1991 to run a newsroom staff of more than 100.

The *Star* won the Pulitzer Prize in 1981 for its investigation of the University of Arizona football program. The news-

paper also has received the nation's highest award for environmental reporting, top honors for public service, and recognition for a report on the North American Free Trade Agreement.

NEWS COVERAGE INSIDE AND OUT

Besides delivery to Tucson's doorsteps, the *Star* and *Citizen* are delivered over the Internet. StarNet at www.azstarnet.com and Southern Arizona Online at www.tucsoncitizen.com offer on-line readers the content of the daily papers as well as special on-line sections, including business directories and real estate information. Entertainment, classified, local news, and sports all are available at the click of a mouse. StarNet also provides its subscribers with award-winning on-line

services such as member home pages and E-mail addresses.

With more than 35,000 visitors daily, these Web sites get more traffic than any other Web site in southern Arizona. Both allow the public to interact with the newspapers' writers and with each other. Tucsonans throughout the city and all over the world can log on every day to see what's going on and to offer their comments and ideas

LOOKING TO THE FUTURE

The Southwest remains one of the fastest-growing regions of the United States, and Tucson is assured of sharing in this exciting expansion. As this trend continues, Tucson Newspapers is committed to being at the forefront of local news media preparing for this growth.

As the size, diversity, and sophistication of Tucson's population has grown, people have relied upon Tucson Newspapers to lead the way in providing for their changing needs. The company has responded to this challenge by expanding its existing products and services and by creating new ones. In addition, Tucson Newspapers has also demonstrated its commitment by recently investing more than $7 million in new printing technology. This new technology has made it possible to deliver four times the number of color pages to its readers.

Also, StarNet has been a new media leader in expanding services to the Internet. As E-commerce emerges, StarNet will help Tucson's small businesses take advantage of the world market and keep consumer spending in the community rather than let it disappear into cyberspace.

Tucson Newspapers is committed to being Tucson's news, information, and media leader. This commitment is clearly demonstrated in the company's mission statement: "In cooperation with *The Arizona Daily Star* and *Tucson Citizen*, Tucson Newspapers is committed to providing products of the highest quality to meet the needs of our readers, advertisers, and employees. We are dedicated to being the leader in our industry through excellence in service, craftsmanship, creativity, and value. We pledge to continue to reflect the diverse community in which we live and uphold the public's trust by maintaining uncompromising standards of integrity and fairness."

C ARONDELET HEALTH NETWORK HAS SERVED SOUTHERN ARIZONA FOR MORE THAN A CENTURY BY PROVIDING QUALITY MEDICAL SERVICES IN A CARING MANNER, FULFILLING THE HEALTH MINISTRY OF THE SISTERS OF ST. JOSEPH OF CARONDELET, AND

strengthening the mission of the Roman Catholic Church.

Carondelet Health Network is a non-profit organization with close to 5,000 employees and some 1,800 physicians and allied professionals on its medical staff. Programs and services include hospice, home health, rehabilitation, occupational health, behavioral health, imaging, and the Healthy Seniors Program.

A STORIED HISTORY

The Sisters of St. Joseph of Carondelet was founded in 1650 in Le Puy, France. In 1870, members of the order traveled to the Arizona Territory, where they opened schools in Tucson and a hospital for injured miners in Prescott.

St. Mary's Hospital opened April 24, 1880, thanks to the efforts of Jean Baptiste Salpointe, vicar apostolic of Arizona. The hospital's first 11 patients arrived May 1, 1880. Salpointe sold St. Mary's to the Sisters of St. Joseph of Carondelet in 1882, with the provision that it always be called St. Mary's and that it be used as a hospital for 99 years.

The only hospital on the southwest side of Tucson, St. Mary's now offers a full range of inpatient and outpatient services. The facility is home to southern Arizona's only burn and wound care program, which recently celebrated its 30th anniversary. Lifeline's emergency response helicopter serves St. Mary's urgent care and emergency department, one of the busiest in Tucson.

ADDITIONAL SITES

In addition to St. Mary's Hospital, Carondelet maintains three facilities in southern Arizona: Carondelet St. Joseph's Hospital, which opened on the east side in 1961; Carondelet Holy Cross Hospital in Nogales, which became part of the network in 1987; and Carondelet Medical Mall in Green Valley, which opened in 1992.

St. Joseph's Hospital continues to provide comprehensive acute care with a focus on outpatient treatment. The Glenn Koepke Urgent Care Center and Emergency Services serves patients on Tucson's east side who need care right away.

Holy Cross Hospital in Nogales has been serving the Santa Cruz County community for more than 100 years, and Carondelet Health Network has sponsored the 80-bed hospital for more than

a decade. The hospital offers an emergency room and maternal/newborn care, as well as laboratory and medical imaging services.

Carondelet Medical Mall offers a range of primary, specialty, and preventive care services under one roof. More than 30 physicians also lease space in the mall.

Other branches of Carondelet include the Carondelet Medical Group, a professional corporation that operates separately from the health network. With nearly 60 physicians and locations in Tucson, Green Valley, and Nogales, Carondelet Medical Group is a gateway for many patients into Carondelet Health Network. The Carondelet Foundation, the network's charitable fund-raising arm, builds supportive relationships through philanthropy, stewardship, and education.

CLOCKWISE FROM TOP: IN 1870, MEMBERS OF THE ORDER OF THE SISTERS OF ST. JOSEPH OF CARONDELET, FOUNDED IN 1650 IN LE PUY, FRANCE, TRAVELED TO THE ARIZONA TERRITORY, WHERE THEY OPENED SCHOOLS IN TUCSON AND A HOSPITAL FOR INJURED MINERS IN PRESCOTT.

ST. JOSEPH'S HOSPITAL PROVIDES COMPREHENSIVE ACUTE CARE WITH A FOCUS ON OUTPATIENT TREATMENT.

ESTABLISHED IN 1880, ST. MARY'S HOSPITAL OFFERS A FULL RANGE OF INPATIENT AND OUTPATIENT SERVICES, AND IS HOME TO SOUTHERN ARIZONA'S ONLY BURN AND WOUND CARE PROGRAM, WHICH RECENTLY CELEBRATED ITS 30TH ANNIVERSARY.

THE UNIVERSITY OF ARIZONA (UA) WAS FOUNDED IN 1885, WHEN THE ARIZONA TERRITORY LEGISLATURE AWARDED A $25,000 APPROPRIATION FOR ITS CREATION AND MANDATED A LAND GRANT FOR THE INSTITUTION. JACOB S. MANSFELD,

a member of the first board of regents, picked out a site for the university about a mile east of Tucson, and convinced its owners, professional gamblers E.B. Gifford and Ben C. Parker, and saloon keeper W.S. "Billy" Read, to donate the land. The deed was filed in 1886, and the university opened it doors on October 1, 1891, with a freshman class of six students.

From this modest start has grown a top-notch, student-centered research institution with an enrollment of 34,327 students drawn from all 50 states and 124 countries. Today, with an internationally known faculty and 120 undergraduate, 121 masters, 91 doctoral, four specialist, and three first professional programs, UA is ranked 16th in academic quality by *U.S. News & World Report* and 10th in spending on research and development by the National Science Foundation among public universities. In addition,

the UA honors program is the second largest in the country.

AN EMPHASIS ON RESEARCH
Renowned for its interdisciplinary scholarship that combines programs such as

medicine and engineering, the university's students and faculty are making some of today's most important scientific discoveries. Students have worked on a range of projects of global importance, including the Imager camera for the recent *Mars*

▼ JOHN FLORENCE

UNIVERSITY OF ARIZONA (UA) STUDENT RICHARD WORKMAN WATCHES A MONITOR SCREEN AS HE ADJUSTS AN ATOMIC FORCE MICROSCOPE. WORKMAN IS PART OF A TEAM INVESTIGATING HOW MOLECULAR STRUCTURES ARE ALTERED BY SURFACE FORCES; THE RESEARCH COULD LEAD TO IMPROVED CLEANING MATERIALS RANGING FROM HOUSEHOLD CLEANERS TO REMOVING OIL FROM POLLUTED WATER.

A STUDENT-CENTERED RESEARCH UNIVERSITY WITH A STUDENT POPULATION OF 35,000, UA HAS OVER THE PAST DECADE RECEIVED MORE THAN $2 BILLION IN RESEARCH GRANTS. THE 352-ACRE INSTITUTION'S TOTAL IMPACT ON SALES IN PIMA COUNTY IS $1.8 BILLION ANNUALLY.

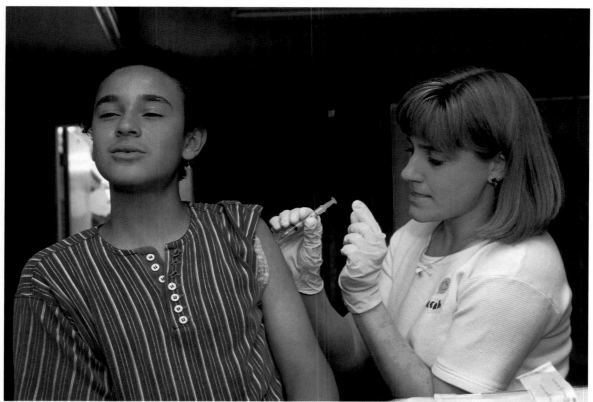

Pathfinder project. The camera took fascinating pictures of the planet's surface for several weeks, winning an award from *Life* magazine, as well as a science photography award from Columbia University. Students also helped analyze the data transmitted by the camera. The space shuttle *Discovery*, which recently carried John Glenn back into space, also carried two UA telescope experiments.

Research grants for the university have totaled more than $2 billion during the past decade, with fellowships and research support coming from such prestigious sources as AT&T, Hughes, NASA, the National Science Foundation, the National Institutes of Health, and the U.S. Air Force. The National Science Foundation recently awarded a $2 million, five-year grant for UA graduate students working at the interface of biology, mathematics, and physics.

COMMUNITY IMPACT

A steady flow of technology, innovation, and ingenuity streaming from UA has infused the Tucson area with pronounced economic growth. UA's total impact on sales in Pima County is $1.8 billion annually.

"If you had to put a price tag on the quality of ideas from faculty, it would be more than $300 million a year," says UA spokeswoman Sharon Kha. One example is the many optics businesses that have spun off from the university's

optics program, which is ranked among the highest in the country. Participants in UA optics programs have started more than 100 companies, generating more than $50 million in local business.

"UA's shift to optics makes us unique," Kha says. "There are 80 companies in this community alone that have been started by our graduates, faculty members, or students."

Knowledge gathered at UA is used to benefit the residents of Arizona in many ways, an objective that has been followed since the university's earliest days. In fact, when UA's first building, Old Main, was built in 1887, it included an atmospheric sciences research lab, and the faculty was charged with the task of supplying climatological information to the state's ranchers and farmers. Recent studies at UA aimed at the community include such topics as the sustainability of water resources in the Tucson Basin.

"Coming from a private university to a land-grant university, I have been struck by the special responsibilities land-grant universities have to the communities in which they live, particularly when it comes to applying knowledge and expertise to a serious community problem," says UA President Peter Likins. "Water resources are clearly a major issue, and we are fortunate at the University of Arizona to have several of the world's leading experts in the field."

PREPARING STUDENTS FOR THE FUTURE

In addition to its outstanding academic programs, UA presents many cultural and athletic opportunities for its students. It houses the Arizona State Museum, UA Museum of Art, and Center for Creative Photography, and maintains several smaller galleries and exhibits on campus. UA has some of the top athletic programs in the nation, including football, softball, baseball, gymnastics, volleyball, soccer, golf, tennis, swimming and diving, and track and field. The men's basketball team won the 1997 NCAA National Championship, and the women's team made the 1998 NCAA Sweet 16.

Located on 352 acres in the heart of Tucson, surrounded by mountains and the high Sonoran Desert, the university continues to improve its campus and its resources for students. Building plans for the university include the new Integrated Learning Center, which will combine classrooms, tutors, advisers, faculty offices, and a computer lab, with the aim of supporting first-year students.

UA has seen stellar growth and change throughout its long history. And for more than a century, the University of Arizona has succeeded in its threefold mission of educating students, conducting significant and scholarly research, and providing public service to the citizens of Tucson and Arizona.

TUCSON ELECTRIC POWER COMPANY (TEP) HAS BEEN PROVIDING ENERGY TO RESIDENTS OF THE TUCSON AREA FOR MORE THAN 100 YEARS, GROWING TO KEEP UP WITH THE BOOMING POPULATION OF THE DESERT. TODAY, THE COMPANY HAS THE CAPACITY TO

distribute nearly 2,000 megawatts of electricity to its 320,000 customers, which include thousands of households and businesses, several copper mines, and two military bases. More than 14,000 miles of high-voltage transmission lines bring power to customers from plants in northern and east-central Arizona and northwestern New Mexico.

"We're defining Tucson Electric Power as a company that will be very responsive to the customer," said Chairman, President, and Chief Executive Officer Jim Pignatelli. "Our objective is to make a long-standing commitment to the consumer, new technology, and the environment."

A HISTORY OF TAKING RISKS
TEP has been well acquainted with the risks businesses need to take to be suc-

cessful. In 1892, despite the failure of an earlier power company, several Tucson citizens decided to take a gamble and form the Electric Light and Power Company to illuminate the city's streets. Prominent merchant Albert Steinfeld was named the first president, and the first power plant was built on North Church Street, across from the Pima County Courthouse. The rate for a house with three lamps was $3 a month.

In 1896, the utility purchased Tucson Gas Company, but the plant was destroyed by a storm two years later. Facing financial problems, TEP was sold to J.J. Henry of Denver in 1901. Soon, U.S. Light and Traction Company of Denver took controlling interest in the utility.

In 1902, the company won a 25-year franchise from the city council and became the Tucson Gas, Electric Light

and Power Company. The company moved its business and production facilities in 1904 to West Sixth Street, the current headquarters.

The company survived the stock market crash of 1929, but utility customers were hurt by the Great Depression, so the company announced rate relief for all 16,000 customers in 1932. A bright spot came in 1933 when Mayor Henry Jaastad marked the arrival of natural gas by igniting a gas torch with a Roman candle.

In 1943, the Securities and Exchange Commission ordered U.S. Light and Traction to divest itself of the company, the same year the company's generating capacity was boosted by hydroelectric power created by the Parker Dam on the Colorado River. The company's common stock was sold to the public in 1946, and by the end of the year, there were 1,927 stockholders from 40 states and the District of Columbia. Tucson residents showed further confidence in Tucson Gas, Electric Light and Power Company in 1951 when they voted to give the company a new, 25-year franchise. In turn, the company agreed to place part of its downtown electrical system underground.

In 1961, the Arizona Corporation Commission awarded the company the first general rate increase in its history. Three years later, the name and domicile of the company changed from Tucson Gas, Electric Light and Power Company, a Colorado corporation, to Tucson Gas and Electric Company, an Arizona corporation.

In 1967, the company's current customer service and administration center opened on West Sixth Street, and two years later, trading began in the company's common stock on the New York Stock Exchange under the symbol TGE. Ten years later, regulatory approval was obtained to build a new, coal-fired generating station near Springerville in east-central Arizona. When the company's gas properties were sold to Southwest Gas Corporation in 1979 for $37 million, the shareholders approved a new name: Tucson Electric Power Company.

By its 100th anniversary in 1992, the company had fought back from losses

◀ JEFF SMITH/FOTOSMITH

MORE THAN 14,000 MILES OF HIGH-VOLTAGE TRANSMISSION LINES BRING POWER TO TUCSON ELECTRIC POWER COMPANY (TEP) CUSTOMERS FROM PLANTS IN NORTHERN AND EAST-CENTRAL ARIZONA AND NORTHWESTERN NEW MEXICO.

TEP HAS BEEN PROVIDING ENERGY TO RESIDENTS OF THE TUCSON AREA FOR MORE THAN 100 YEARS, GROWING TO KEEP UP WITH THE BOOMING POPULATION OF THE DESERT.

with a major financial restructuring plan, while at the same time managing to provide stable, reliable electric service. TEP's holding company, UniSource Energy Corporation, began trading on the New York Stock Exchange in January 1998.

A PARTNER IN THE COMMUNITY

TEP is committed to building a stronger community through corporate leadership and commitment of resources to customer communities. The company annually invests approximately $2 million in the Pima County and White Mountain communities through grants, volunteerism, educational programs, and in-kind contributions.

TEP feels a responsibility to the community to take care of its citizens and customers, and community partnerships are important to it as a means to address critical social problems. The Driving Drunk Will Put Your Lights Out campaign was enacted to prevent impaired driving, and the Healthy Families campaign was initiated to prevent child abuse and to promote positive parenting.

The Community Action Team (CAT) is TEP's company volunteer program. In 1997, 32 percent of TEP employees volunteered with their families, giving an

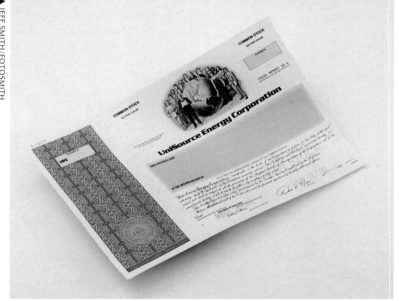

estimated 9,000 volunteer hours to more than 200 Arizona nonprofit organizations.

READY FOR NEW CHALLENGES

Today, TEP faces new challenges, including deregulation of the utility industry. "The company will be smaller, more efficient, and more focused on consumer goods," Pignatelli says. "We'll help customers get more value for their energy dollar."

Changes in the utility industry will also include better technology, more direct access to power sources, and more consumer control over how that power is used. TEP also is investing heavily in environmentally friendly methods of producing energy.

Yet, despite all the uncertainty in the industry, Pignatelli is confident that the company will continue to grow. "We're not afraid of reinventing our business," he says. "We believe it is essential to our survival."

TEP'S PARENT COMPANY, UNISOURCE ENERGY CORPORATION, BEGAN TRADING ON THE NEW YORK STOCK EXCHANGE IN JANUARY 1998.

BEFORE THE ARIZONA TERRITORY ACHIEVED STATEHOOD IN 1912, EVERYTHING IMPORTANT CAME TO TUCSON BY TRAIN. CITIZENS TRANSFER & STORAGE CO., INC., WHICH WAS FOUNDED IN 1907, WAS THE NEXT STEP IN THE PROCESS: USING TRUCKS, THE

company transported goods from the train station to customers throughout the community. Today, the company is the oldest in Tucson, and one of few that have been operating continuously since Arizona became the 48th state.

Today, Citizens Transfer maintains three warehouses around the Greater Tucson area, and specializes in moving households, offices, and commercial products, as well as a variety of other services. "We make efforts to go after corporate and private business as well as households," says President E.W. Belton.

A FAMILY BUSINESS

Edward R. Belton, E.W. Belton's father, began working at Citizens Transfer in 1921 after graduating from the University of Arizona (UA). By the late 1920s, he had become half owner, and eventually bought the entire firm and became its president. In 1931, Citizens Transfer became one of the original agents for Allied Van Lines, an interstate mover of household goods. The business survived the Great Depression

and, during World War II, picked up contracts to relocate people at Fort Huachuca and Davis-Monthan Air Force Base. The Citizens Transfer office in Sierra Vista continues to serve the Fort Huachuca area.

E.W. Belton took over as president in 1984. Also a UA graduate, Belton first worked for the company in the warehouse. Today, his son, John, and one of his daughters, Mary Ann, work for Citizens Transfer as well. "We've had the same family running the business since 1921," Belton says. "We have a desire to improve our service to our customers and perform our services for a fair cost and at a fair return for good service."

BRANCHING OUT

In addition to its fleet of 60 trucks dedicated to residential moves throughout the United States and Canada, Citizens Transfer today offers a wide range of services. Its three commercial warehouses store all sorts of products and materials for businesses throughout the Tucson area. The warehouses, which have fire sprinklers

and are monitored electronically, are served by rail sidings that can accommodate up to 12 railcars and have 15 semi-truck bays. Citizens Transfer also stores business records, which are indexed by computer and bar-coded for rapid identification.

Other services and facilities include certified records destruction and a climate-controlled, fire-resistant vault for storing sensitive electronic media. The company is also skilled at relocating businesses, with a move counselor on staff to help plan the transition and workers who are skilled at transporting everything from sensitive computer equipment to heavy safes.

According to Belton, among the company's greatest assets are its workers, who are able to respond to the constantly shifting demands of their jobs. "We have a very, very solid crew of employees," Belton says. "We have an interesting business. There's never one day where anything is the same. We may have 25 customers in one day. There's not a one of them that has the same needs."

E.W. BELTON TOOK OVER AS PRESIDENT OF CITIZENS TRANSFER & STORAGE CO., INC. IN 1984. TODAY, HIS SON, JOHN, AND ONE OF HIS DAUGHTERS, MARY ANN, WORK FOR CITIZENS TRANSFER AS WELL. "WE'VE HAD THE SAME FAMILY RUNNING THE BUSINESS SINCE 1921," BELTON SAYS. "WE HAVE A DESIRE TO IMPROVE OUR SERVICE TO OUR CUSTOMERS AND PERFORM OUR SERVICES FOR A FAIR COST AND AT A FAIR RETURN FOR GOOD SERVICE."

W

ITH THE LATEST IN HIGH-TECH, HIGH-QUALITY EQUIPMENT AND A CREW OF DEDICATED REPORTERS, KOLD-TV NEWS 13 SERVES THE ENTIRE SOUTHERN ARIZONA REGION WITH SERIOUS, HARD-HITTING NEWS COVERAGE. ■ THE FIRST

television station in Tucson, KOLD-TV first went on the air on January 31, 1953, as KOPO-TV, under the ownership of the Old Pueblo Broadcasting Company. Today, the station is a CBS affiliate and is part of Raycom Media, a Montgomery, Alabama-based media company with more than 32 television stations across the country.

LIVE. LOCAL. LATEBREAKING.

The KOLD-TV News 13 crew lives by the station's slogan, presenting news that is "Live. Local. Latebreaking." With News 13 This Morning, News 13 at Noon, News 13 at Five, News 13 at 5:30, News 13 at Six, and News 13 at Ten, KOLD-TV strives to give the southern Arizona community vital and important news that affects every resident.

"We care about what happens to the people in our community," says Mindy Blake, News 13 anchor. "That's why we

focus on issues that affect our viewers—health, parenting, consumer news—as well as everyday news that touches our lives."

STAYING AHEAD OF THE PACK

In February 1998, KOLD-TV debuted its newest feature, Chopper 13, becoming the first station to cover Tucson from above with live broadcasts. A Bell JetRanger III, Chopper 13 is equipped with global positioning and microwave transmitter technology, which allows for air-to-ground and audiovisual communication. Chopper 13 provides Tucsonans a different perspective on the city and on the news.

News 13 broadcasts also feature a number of unique segments that provide viewers with useful, up-to-the-minute information. For instance, HealthBeat, hosted by News 13 anchor Barbara Grijalva and registered nurse Peggy Pico, airs

three times a day and covers the latest health and medical news.

With studios in northwest Tucson, KOLD-TV maintains top-of-the-line news reporting equipment, all to bring important news to viewers more quickly and efficiently. The station uses three Panasonic 3CCD digital cameras in the studio, and its photojournalists use Panasonic DVC Pro cameras when reporting live throughout the region. In addition, Emmy Award-winning graphic artist Todd Ailts designs the station's logos and graphics in-house. KOLD-TV also houses a state-of-the-art non-linear editing facility with an AVID Media Composer 1000 for commercial and promotional production.

As it reports news that is vital to the region, KOLD-TV News 13 is sure to be part of southern Arizona's future, striving to serve the needs of the community it has called home for nearly 50 years.

▲ CAREY HAAS

WITH STUDIOS IN NORTHWEST TUCSON, KOLD-TV MAINTAINS TOP-OF-THE-LINE NEWS REPORTING EQUIPMENT, ALL TO BRING IMPORTANT NEWS TO VIEWERS MORE QUICKLY AND EFFICIENTLY (TOP).

KOLD-TV NEWS 13'S ANCHORS— INCLUDING (FROM LEFT) KRIS PICKEL, RANDY GARSEE, MINDY BLAKE, AND BARBARA GRIJALVA—DELIVER NEWS THAT IS "LIVE. LOCAL. LATEBREAKING. (BOTTOM)"

INNER OF *INDUSTRY WEEK* MAGAZINE'S AMERICA'S BEST PLANT AWARD IN 1999, RAYTHEON MISSILE SYSTEMS HAS THE WEIGHTY RESPONSIBILITY OF HELPING TO ENSURE THE SAFETY OF MILITARY MEN AND WOMEN AROUND THE WORLD.

"A missile may never get used, but if it's ever called upon to defend someone, it has to work. It's of national importance," says Jerry Lockard, vice president of missile systems in Tucson. "You don't know until you pull the trigger whether it's going to fly or not. They have to work every time, all the time, the first time."

DEEP ROOTS IN TUCSON

Raytheon is the largest private sector employer in Tucson and southern Arizona, with 9,500 workers. Over the years, the company has delivered more than 1 million defense products, while keeping a focus on customer service and quality. The Tucson facility was built in 1951 by Howard Hughes, and first manufactured air-to-air Falcon missiles for the U.S. Air Force. The Hughes Aircraft Company operation remained at the site for 48

years, with employment peaking in 1985 at more than 9,000 workers. But as the cold war wound down, missile demand dropped too, and by 1992, the number of employees had fallen to 3,900.

"Hughes was faced with a choice to buy or sell a missile business," Lockard says. Hughes decided to buy General Dynamics' California-based missile business, which made systems like the Rolling Airframe Missile (RAM), as well as the Sparrow, Stinger, Standard, Tomahawk, and Advanced Cruise missiles. After the purchase in late 1992, about 3,000 families moved from California to Tucson, and around the same time, the Tucson facility was changed into a center of excellence for designing and manufacturing. Hughes won contracts for systems like the next-generation Sidewinder air-to-air missile, and the Evolved SeaSparrow,

Tomahawk, and Phalanx missiles.

"We were doing very well here in Tucson, with the manufacturing base and the strong engineering base," Lockard says.

But further cuts to the nation's defense budget prompted Hughes to again decide to either buy or sell. This time, Hughes sold the firm's aerospace portion to Raytheon in December 1997.

Such moves are designed to eliminate redundancy and increase efficiency, and there were a few tense months as the Tucson facility waited to hear whether it would survive the merger. "We were sort of sitting on pins and needles, wondering where we would go," Lockard says. In the end, Raytheon decided to move its missile business from Massachusetts to Tucson, bringing with it projects like the Advanced Medium-Range Air-to-Air

EACH YEAR, RAYTHEON MISSILE SYSTEMS EMPLOYEES HELP RESTORE HOMES FOR LOW-INCOME RESIDENTS, THE ELDERLY, AND PEOPLE WITH DISABILITIES IN THE TUCSON AREA.

Missile (AMRAAM), as well as the Standard, Maverick, and Sparrow missiles. "They brought five programs here and made us competitive and more cost-effective," Lockard says.

Raytheon also closed its Texas facilities in 1998 and moved to Tucson projects like the Joint Standoff Weapon system, the Javelin antitank missile, the High-Speed Antiradiation Missile (HARM), and the Paveway precision guided weapons, many of which were used in the 1999 Kosovo conflict. With those projects came hundreds of well-educated workers who helped boost Tucson's economy even more, with a total Raytheon payroll of about $500 million in 1999.

THE BEST IN TACTICAL MISSILE DEVELOPMENT

Raytheon spends more than $100 million annually on its 500 suppliers in Arizona, with about $80 million of that spent in Tucson, and also uses about 4 million square feet of floor space locally.

Fifteen major missile programs are now in production in Tucson, with 16 initiatives in development. Among its current production programs are AMRAAM ("the weapon of choice for air force and navy air-to-air capability," comments Lockard); Maverick, RAM, Stinger, and Tomahawk missiles; the Tube-launched, Optically tracked, Wire-guided (TOW) missile; and the Advanced Short-Range Air-to-Air Missile (ASRAAM).

"Our charter is to be the best in tactical missile development," Lockard says. "We cover all kinds of technology. We're an industry leader in radar and infrared technology, and we are systems engineers. We are number one and that's where we want to stay."

The company serves a broad base of U.S. and international customers. "For us to continue to grow, we have to grow internationally," Lockard adds. "There are many opportunities with our allies."

STRIVING FOR EXCELLENCE

Raytheon employees contribute tens of thousands of volunteer hours every year to the Tucson community. The com-

pany takes part in the Christmas in April building project each year, and its employees make the largest single contribution to the United Way of Greater Tucson, giving about $1 million each year.

In 1997, the company won the prestigious Arizona Governor's Award for Quality, as well as the Best Manufacturing Practices Award from the U.S. Navy in 1998. The navy named 84 Raytheon practices the best in the industry, the most ever included in the award.

In 1999, Raytheon also won the America's Best Plant Award from *Industry Week* magazine, beating out 419 competitors to finish as the largest employer in the top 10. The Arizona Board of Regents also honored Raytheon in 1999 for its outstanding contributions to higher education.

"As these awards indicate, we're very focused on customer satisfaction, as well as quality, competitiveness, and financial health," says Lockard. "We spend a lot of time with the workforce, making them feel like they're a team, making them feel like the best in what we're doing."

ITH DEREGULATION ON THE HORIZON FOR TUCSONANS, THE DAYS OF HAVING NO CHOICE OF ELECTRIC SUPPLIERS WILL SOON BE OVER. ONE ELECTRIC SUPPLIER, SIERRA SOUTH-WEST ELECTRIC POWER COOPERATIVE SERVICES, INC.,

is working hard to make sure its services will be part of Tucson's future. As a cooperative, Sierra Southwest ensures reasonable prices, and more importantly, it is owned and controlled by its customers.

Sierra Southwest and its members are among the nation's electric cooperatives leading the charge to build a national brand: Touchstone Energy. Touchstone Energy serves as a brand identity and marketing umbrella for more than 560 local customer-owned cooperatives nationwide, and it strives to uphold four values: integrity, accountability, innovation, and commitment to community. Touchstone Energy serves more than 4.7 million households and businesses, reaching more than 12 million people in 40 states. Its slogan sums up its philosophy: Deregulation gives you a choice, Touchstone Energy gives you a voice. The company has one loyalty, and that's to the customer.

In addition to marketing, Touchstone Energy also provides access to other resources, such as natural gas and energy management services. "In some cases, we'll install on-site generation or equipment that will guarantee power quality,"

explains Dennis Criswell, assistant general manager of marketing and customer service for Sierra Southwest. "We are also looking at providing long-distance phone services. Since we're owned by the customers, we'll do whatever the customers want. We're not selling electricity; we're selling cooperatives. We're selling a way of doing business."

Sierra Southwest is made up of six electric cooperatives, including Trico Electric, which serves rural areas surrounding Tucson. Trico's more than 22,000 members range from residences in SaddleBrooke on the city's northwest side to Ski Valley on top of Mount Lemmon. Other members include the Pinal County Air Park, the Army National Guard Training Center, and outlying communities like Arivaca with farms and ranches near the Mexican border. "Cooperatives have always had a diverse mixture of customers," Criswell says.

Regulations allow Arizonans to choose which energy company they want to supply them with power, with choices between investor-owned and customer-owned utilities. Sierra Southwest and Trico Electric,

which was founded in 1945, are two of those choices in Tucson.

A LONG HISTORY
Cooperatives have a rich history in America. The nation's first cooperative, which provided fire insurance, was founded by Benjamin Franklin. Power cooperatives, in particular, have been doing business since the 1930s, when the Rural Electrification Administration provided loans for rural electric cooperatives to build power distribution systems and small generating facilities. This helped bring power to rural ranches and farms, many of which had no electricity even after the nation's cities were lit up. By definition, cooperative utilities are locally owned, and their boards of directors are made up of and elected by customers. Besides their focus on customers, electric cooperatives are similar to not-for-profit corporations.

A LOCAL CONNECTION
In 1961, Trico Electric and three other rural electric distribution cooperatives in southeast Arizona banded together to

TOUCHSTONE ENERGY COOPERATIVES IN TUCSON FOCUS ON HELPING COMMUNITIES, AS DEMONSTRATED BY THE COMPANY'S SPONSORSHIP OF THE TOUCHSTONE ENERGY TUCSON OPEN. THE TOURNAMENT NOT ONLY RAISES MONEY FOR WORTHY CAUSES, BUT IT GENERATES LOCAL REVENUE.

form Arizona Electric Power Cooperative, Inc. (AEPCO), a generation and transmission cooperative. AEPCO's customers range from the farmlands and copper mines of southern Arizona to the retirement communities and tourist attractions along the Colorado River to the booming Tucson suburbs. Headquartered in Benson, 45 miles southeast of Tucson, AEPCO's Apache Generating Station in Cochise has the ability to generate 520 megawatts per hour. This power plant is the primary source of electricity sold by Trico and Sierra Southwest.

In addition to their commitment to customers, Touchstone Energy cooperatives in Tucson focus on helping communities, as demonstrated by the company's sponsorship of the Touchstone Energy Tucson Open. The tournament not only raises money for worthy causes, but it generates local revenue. Touchstone Energy also is the title sponsor for the state high schools' all-star games, which involve nearly every community in the state.

AEPCO has developed the Apache Station Wildlife Viewing Area in wetlands near the generating station in Cochise. Created in the 1980s, the viewing area is a seasonal home to sandhill cranes, bald and golden eagles, and other wildlife. The cooperative offers tours and has built roads and a handicapped-accessible viewing area.

It's all part of a cooperative's commitment to its customers and its communities. Says Criswell, "Since we are owned by the people who live there, we want to make certain the communities in which we live and the communities where we serve folks are successful."

THROUGH ITS DISPATCH CENTER AND ON-SITE MAINTENANCE CREWS, ARIZONA ELECTRIC POWER COOPERATIVE, INC. SERVES CUSTOMERS FROM THE FARMLANDS AND COPPER MINES OF SOUTHERN ARIZONA TO THE RETIREMENT COMMUNITIES AND TOURIST ATTRACTIONS ALONG THE COLORADO RIVER TO THE BOOMING TUCSON SUBURBS (TOP LEFT AND RIGHT).

HEADQUARTERED IN BENSON, 45 MILES SOUTHEAST OF TUCSON, AEPCO'S APACHE GENERATING STATION IN COCHISE HAS THE ABILITY TO GENERATE 520 MEGAWATTS PER HOUR. THIS POWER PLANT IS THE PRIMARY SOURCE OF ELECTRICITY SOLD BY TRICO AND SIERRA SOUTHWEST ELECTRIC POWER COOPERATIVE SERVICES, INC. (BOTTOM).

FROM ITS HUMBLE BEGINNINGS IN AN IOWA GARAGE TO TODAY'S MODERN INDUSTRIAL PLANT IN TUCSON, MILES LABEL COMPANY, INC. BRINGS TO MIND ONE IMPORTANT WORD: FAMILY. WHEN RUSSELL HUBERT MILES BEGAN RUNNING A PRINTING

operation out of his Des Moines garage in 1912, he started a family legacy that lives on nearly nine decades later. By 1930, he and his son Paul Wilson Miles were printing labels and creating such specialty items as policy labels and business forms for insurance companies.

To escape the harsh Iowa winters, Paul and his son, Robert, moved the company's operations and six of its employees to Tucson in 1962, and by 1966, Paul had officially joined the firm. Miles Label Company set up shop in a downtown building near the corner of Flores Street and Stone Avenue and stayed there until 1985, when it moved to its current site in the Continental Ranch Business Park. Coincidentally, the company has always been located near a soft drink plant. "Something sweet brings good luck to the business," says P.J. Miles, the company's secretary-treasurer, part owner, and Paul's son. "Since we moved in 1962, the company's now handling 10 times the volume of business."

Also helping to run Miles Label Company is Jim Lupori, vice president and partner in sales. And from 1950 until his

retirement in 1989, Paul's father, Robert H. Miles, was heavily involved in the business as well. "Turnover has been low at the company, and that's because it's a family business," P.J. says. "We want all our employees to feel they play an important role in the growth of the company."

FUTURE OF LABELS

Today, the 18 employees of Miles Label Company use many types of papers, adhesives, and films in order to manufacture labels for products ranging from cosmetics to salsa. The company also prints prescription labels and bar codes, as well as labels for weapons such as bombs and grenades for ordnance companies. Some of the company's ordnance labels bind weapons together until they are ready for use, while its grenade labels incorporate instructions on how to use them.

Although most of its clients are based in Arizona, many others call on Miles Label Company's specialized expertise from across the United States, including 22-year customer Kimberly-

Clark. According to Paul, the company's focus on labels differentiates it from others in the diverse printing industry. "There are so many different aspects to printing," he explains, "so we are focusing on becoming the best we can possibly be to satisfy our customers' labeling needs."

A member of the Tucson Printers Association, Miles Label Company designs and typesets products using Macintosh computers equipped with state-of-the-art software. The company's equipment can produce business forms and collate up to an eight-part form, and with six-color presses and a modern platemaker, the quality of the labels is better than ever.

Looking back at its strong performance in the past, Miles Label Company projects that its history of expansion will continue over the next several years. Based on the growing need for labels across a variety of business sectors, this Tucson company plans to further diversify its offerings. "Walk through a grocery store and look at how many labels are on everything," P.J. says. "The need is growing daily."

MILES LABEL COMPANY, INC. USES MANY TYPES OF PAPERS, ADHESIVES, AND FILMS TO MANUFACTURE LABELS FOR PRODUCTS RANGING FROM COSMETICS TO SALSA. THE COMPANY ALSO PRINTS PRESCRIPTION LABELS AND BAR CODES, AS WELL AS LABELS FOR WEAPONS SUCH AS BOMBS AND GRENADES FOR ORDNANCE COMPANIES.

HE STATE OF ARIZONA HAS ONLY ONE RESIDENT PROFESSIONAL THEATER COMPANY—BUT, SURPRISINGLY, ITS HOME BASE ISN'T THE CAPITAL CITY. BASED IN TUCSON, ARIZONA THEATRE COMPANY (ATC) PRESENTS PRIZEWINNING WORKS BY

playwrights ranging from William Shakespeare to Tom Stoppard, performing six plays annually for more than 150,000 patrons in Tucson and Phoenix.

ATC is the only regional theater company in the United States that performs in two cities. Each year, the company holds its season opening in Tucson in the historic Temple of Music and Art. "No company could ask for a better, more welcoming home in which to present its work," says Artistic Director David Ira Goldstein. The play then moves to the Herberger Theater Center in Phoenix. "The company really does take seriously its role as a state theater," adds Goldstein. "It's our job to serve the whole state."

ATC was founded in Tucson by Sandy Rosenthal in 1967 as the Arizona Civic Theatre. The theater company, whose operating costs are met by ticket sales and contributions, is dedicated to serving the community as a resource. The company not only strives to keep its ticket prices low, but also offers discounts to students, seniors, and military personnel, as well as accessibility services to hearing and visually impaired communities.

EDUCATION IN THE ARTS
The company has introduced thousands of young people to the theater through its Summer on Stage and Student Matinee programs. Student matinees are available at a discount and scholarships are provided to those who can't afford tickets. Teachers receive study guides for their classes, and students get to talk with the cast following the performance.

ATC also has internship programs with the University of Arizona (UA) and Stephen F. Austin State University in Texas, providing educational opportunities for budding artists, production managers, and administrators. UA students serve as understudies throughout the season, working with some of the nation's top artists, and Austin interns spend an entire year with the company, receiving hands-on training in production and administration.

"I would hope we would play some role in the growth of arts education. Arts education is such a key part of any community, and an endangered one," says Managing Director Jessica L. Andrews.

The company's existing pool of talent, as well as the beauty of the Southwest, helps lure people to the organization. "We have an ability to attract world-class artists, designers, actors, and directors," says Goldstein. ATC's actors are seen on TV, in films, and on the Broadway stage. The company's costume, scene, and property shops build nearly all the costumes, sets, and props used in its productions. ATC is also served by a professional administrative staff, which handles box-office, accounting, fund-raising, marketing, and

other management activities.

In future seasons, Arizona Theatre Company plans to produce more new work. "The mission of the theater has been remarkably consistent: to do a wide variety of work in the best way," says Goldstein. "Our communities here in the Southwest—the uniqueness, the diversity—are something we try to reflect in our repertoire, our staff, and our board. Our audience will continue to grow and diversify, which will allow us to provide a wider palette of experiences."

BASED IN TUCSON, ARIZONA THEATRE COMPANY PRESENTS PRIZE-WINNING WORKS BY PLAYWRIGHTS RANGING FROM WILLIAM SHAKESPEARE TO TOM STOPPARD, PERFORMING SIX PLAYS ANNUALLY FOR MORE THAN 150,000 PATRONS IN TUCSON AND PHOENIX.

SLONE BROADCASTING IS A FAMILY BUSINESS IN EVERY WAY. THE COMPANY IS OWNED AND OPERATED BY A FAMILY. IT IS COMMITTED TO TRUE FAMILY VALUES. BUT MAKE NO MISTAKE ABOUT IT, THIS FAMILY BUSINESS IS NOT A TYPICAL

MAX AND MARY, HOSTS OF THE NUMBER-ONE-RATED MORNING SHOW ON KIIM-FM, SUPPORT THE SLONE BROADCASTING VISION: "TO BE THE STATIONS OF CHOICE BY BUILDING AND SUSTAINING RELATIONSHIPS WITH OUR LISTENERS, ADVERTISERS, COMMUNITY, AND EACH OTHER (TOP)."

SLONE BROADCASTING IS A FAMILY BUSINESS IN EVERY WAY. COMMITTED TO TRUE FAMILY VALUES, THE COMPANY IS OWNED AND OPERATED BY A FAMILY, INCLUDING (FROM LEFT) FRED SLONE, NATIONAL SALES MANAGER; NORMA SLONE; JIM SLONE, PRESIDENT; JAMIE SLONE, VICE PRESIDENT AND GENERAL MANAGER; MARY SLONE-WAMBACH, COHOST OF KIIM-FM'S MORNING SHOW; AND JOE WAMBACH, DIRECTOR OF CLIENT SERVICES (BOTTOM).

mom-and-pop operation. This family business owns and operates five state-of-the-art radio stations in Tucson, including the most listened-to radio station in the city. When it comes to radio, Slone Broadcasting means business.

The success of this family business is the direct result of President Jim Slone's commitment to excellence, quality pro-

gramming, and uncompromising dedication to family values. "We are guests, invited into people's cars, homes, and businesses," Slone says. "We're very careful about the music we play and the things we say because we want to be invited back. This respect for the listeners is the cornerstone of what our radio stations are all about."

"Let me give you an example of how deeply this concept of respect has permeated our company," says Vice President and General Manager Jamie Slone, Jim's son. "We recently asked our employees to help create a vision statement for Slone Broadcasting. The result was this: 'Our Vision: To be the stations of choice by building and sustaining relationships with our listeners, advertisers, community, and each other.' It's very gratifying to see the same kind of core values that my dad stuck to while he was building the company being reflected now by the whole staff."

A FAMILY OPERATION

Almost everyone in the Slone family is involved with the operation of the company's five radio stations. Jamie Slone is the general manager; Jim's youngest son, Fred, is the national sales manager; and daughter Mary Slone-Wambach is half of the number-one-rated Max and Mary morning show on KIIM-FM. In addition, Mary's husband, Joe Wambach, is the company director of client services

It wasn't always this way. The Slone Broadcasting family business started with Jim Slone's move to Tucson from Albuquerque in 1963. The native of Portales, New Mexico, took a job as morning disc jockey for KHOS 940 AM. Through the years, he worked his way up to the position of general manager, and in 1972, was approached by the owners of another local station, KCUB 1290 AM, which was languishing in the ratings. The group asked him to run the station. Slone agreed to take the new job under the condition that he could buy stock in the company.

Under Jim's guidance, KCUB succeeded beyond everyone's expectations, and eventually, after purchasing part of the company, Slone became sole owner of the most listened-to station in town.

KCUB's success reached its highest level in 1976 when it was named the number one country station in America by *Billboard* magazine. KCUB also received the Billboard Award for Grand International Station of the Year. Out of all the radio stations in the world, regardless of city, size, or format, KCUB was judged the best. It was the first and only time any station outside the top 10 markets had won that award.

In 1983, Slone acquired what is now KIIM-FM 99.5, now the flagship station of Slone Broadcasting. By 1993, approximately one out of every three people in Tucson was listening to their country favorites on KIIM. The incredible loyalty and sheer size of the KIIM audience gave the station the highest percentage of listenership in any of the top 70 markets in the country.

REACHING MORE LISTENERS

KIIM-FM remains the most popular station in Tucson, reaching more adult listeners than any other station in the area at any time of the day or night. Herb Crowe,

CHRIS MOONEY/BALFOUR WALKER STUDIOS

vice president of programming for Slone Broadcasting, says, "It's amazing, but KIIM-FM has been the most listened-to radio station with listeners age 25 and older since 1988. That's incredible. There's no doubt that Jim Slone set the standard for country music in Tucson."

In 1992, Federal Communications Commission (FCC) deregulation allowed local owners to own two FM stations and two AM stations in the same town. "We knew in Tucson there was one remaining big signal that had yet to make it to the airwaves," Jamie Slone says. "The FCC had awarded the license, but the station had not yet come on the air, so we found the owner and bought the station from him. In 1995, we turned the station on." The third Slone Broadcasting station was given the call letters KHYT, is known as K-HIT 107.5, and plays classic hit songs from the 1970s.

K-HIT has an uncontested franchise in the Tucson market and is the only radio station specializing in the classic hits of the late 1960s, 1970s, and the early 1980s. The Arbitron Ratings Company recently recognized the station as one of the 10 most successful stations of its type in the United States. "A lot of people were very excited to hear a format they hadn't heard for a long time," Jamie Slone says. "In its first full Arbitron rating period, it was the second-most-listened-to station in Tucson. No other station we know about has achieved such a level of listening at the debut. KIIM was number one and K-HIT was number two, so that was a good day for Slone Broadcasting."

EXPANSION THROUGH ACQUISITION

As the deregulation of ownership rules by the FCC continued, Jamie Slone seized the opportunity to grow Slone Broadcasting with the acquisitions of KTUC-AM and KSJM-FM in 1997.

KSJM-FM was changed from a hip-hop and rap station called Power 97.5 to a smooth jazz station with the call letters KOAZ-FM, and 97.5 The Oasis was born. Conceived and designed for an adult audience with sophisticated musical tastes, the station features a blend of contemporary jazz and adult contemporary music. Many technical improvements were made to maximize the reach and sound quality of the station for the benefit of the especially discriminating audience of the Oasis.

The controversial and struggling talk format of KTUC-AM was jettisoned in favor of a music-intensive approach featuring the popular music of the 1950s,

with just a few songs from the late 1940s and early 1960s.

As a result of this growth, nearly one-half of all the adults in Tucson between the ages of 25 and 54 invite a Slone Broadcasting station into their homes, cars, or workplaces to entertain and inform them each week. The company's diversity in musical formats is meeting the needs, in one way or another, of a vast audience with widely varying tastes.

Being a true family business, Slone Broadcasting differs from most other broadcast groups in Tucson in that the company's sole focus is Tucson. "The fact that the Slone family is not interested in expanding the company to other radio markets allows everyone here to concentrate all the effort and resources on these stations," says Crowe.

CHRIS MOONEY/BALFOUR WALKER STUDIOS

"All the other companies in town have to keep an eye on their corporate strategies, which may mean their stations are sold to another company to benefit the shareholders. That's good for the shareholders, but where is the benefit for the listeners or the community?"

COMMUNITY INVOLVEMENT

Another facet of being a locally owned, family-oriented company is the opportunity to help the community service groups and organizations that serve the people of Tucson. Jim's wife, Norma Slone, set the early standard for the company through her energetic involvement with many philanthropic undertakings. The amount of airtime given to promote the dozens of large and small events over the years would be valued in the millions of dollars.

Each of the five stations appeals to a different group of listeners, and each different audience represents a different opportunity for involvement. For the past several years, KIIM-FM has generated thousands of dollars for Comstock Children's Foundation with its annual KIIM-FM Penny Pitch, a listener-driven penny drive with an annual goal of 1 million pennies. This goal has been exceeded every year, thanks to the gen-

erosity of Tucsonans. The event has proved so successful that KIIM-FM has helped the foundation set up similar events in Phoenix and Yuma, with other cities now in the planning stages.

The KIIM-FM commitment to the community goes beyond that one event and touches national organizations like the annual KIIM-FM Country Auction for the Muscular Dystrophy Association, the American Cancer Society's Relay for Life, the March of Dimes' WalkAmerica, and this past year, the Children's Miracle

Network telethon.

On the local level, KIIM-FM actively promotes and supports the efforts of service groups like the Sunrise Rotary, which produces the annual Fiesta de la Tierra trail ride. KIIM-FM is also a participating sponsor in the Fort Lowell Shootout, an invitational youth soccer tournament that brings 6,000 to 8,000 players of all ages from all over the world to Tucson.

Over the years, the station has also spearheaded fund-raising efforts for in-

KIIM-FM'S MAX AND MARY HOST THE MOST LISTENED-TO MORNING SHOW IN TUCSON.

KIIM-FM IS A MAJOR PART OF TUCSON'S NIGHTLIFE.

dividual families caught in tragic circumstances, and has even reached down to the ultimate grassroots level to help reunite lost dogs, cats, pigs, cows, and horses with their rightful owners.

IT IS A FAMILY BUSINESS

Slone Broadcasting is owned by a family and operated by a family, and each radio station's listeners are treated with the respect of a family member.

Jamie Slone is carrying on the values established by his father. Today, Jim chooses the music for KCUB and KTUC, but leaves most of the day-to-day operation of the company to the rest of the family.

Jim Slone is the only active radio broadcaster in Tucson to be recognized by the Tucson Ad Club for a lifetime of achievement in advertising, marketing, and broadcasting. "The best thing I ever did was to stay in Tucson," he says. "I came in when the population was around 250,000, and as the town got bigger, I grew along with it."

AS PART OF THE PEOPLE OF SLONE BROADCASTING'S (BOTTOM) COMMITMENT TO THE COMMUNITY, JAMIE SLONE DISCUSSED RADIO BROADCASTING WITH TUCSON JUNIOR HIGH SCHOOL STUDENTS (TOP LEFT), AND MAX AND MARY GAVE A SPECIAL TOUR OF THE KIIM-FM STUDIO TO STUDENTS FROM FLOWING WELLS JUNIOR HIGH (TOP RIGHT).

FROM THE VAST REACHES OF OUTER SPACE TO MICROSCOPIC COMPUTER CHIPS, INFRARED LABORATORIES, INC. (IR LABS) HAS HELPED INCREASE SOCIETY'S UNDERSTANDING OF THE UNIVERSE. "NATURE HIDES HER SECRETS IN VARIOUS WAYS, AND A LOT OF

them are hidden in the infrared spectrum," says IR Labs President Frank Low. "We provide the tools that infrared astronomers use to locate and understand such things as how stars and planets are formed, a process that's invisible to ordinary telescopes."

In 1961, while a research scientist at Texas Instruments, Inc., Low developed a new type of infrared detector, the low-temperature germanium bolometer. The new detector drew the attention of astronomers who hoped to use it to explore the sky at uncharted infrared wavelengths. In 1964, Low became a research professor at the Lunar and Planetary Laboratory of the University of Arizona. Responding to his colleagues' interest in his bolometer, Low and his wife, Edith, founded Infrared Laboratories in 1967.

Today, the company designs and builds cutting-edge cryogenic and infrared instrumentation, and trains its customers to use their instruments. "We provide an educational service along with the hardware," Low says. "And we learn from our customers; that's why we're still successful after 32 years."

Since IR Labs was founded, gross sales have increased from $10,000 annually to approximately $5 million in 1999. To accommodate this steady growth, the company moved in October 1979 to its current facility, which has since been expanded several times. One mile south of the University of Arizona, the lab houses manufacturing and test facilities that can achieve very low temperatures. Also, one of the 13 infrared microscopes

(FROM LEFT) INFARED LABORATORIES INC. (IR LABS) VICE PRESIDENT STEVE ZOLTOWSKI, INSTRUMENT MAKER MITCH NASH, AND VICE PRESIDENT ELLIOTT SOLHEID ARE RESPONSIBLE FOR MANY OF THE COMPANYS' INNOVATIVE PRODUCTS, INCLUDING (FROM LEFT) AN ASTRONOMI-CAL CAMERA, A BOLOMETER SYSTEM FOR CHEMICAL ANALYSIS, AND AN LHE3 CRYOSTAT FOR MATERIALS STUDIES AT MINUS 491.5 DEGREES FAHRENHEIT.

IR LABS' INFRARED EMISSION MICRO-SCOPE (IREM1) USES INFRARED DETECTORS DEVELOPED BY THE UNIVERSITY OF ARIZONA FOR NASA'S *HUBBLE SPACE TELESCOPE*. EQUIPPED WITH THESE DETECTORS, THE UNIVER-SITY'S NEAR-INFRARED CAMERA AND MULTI-OBJECT SPECTROMETER (NICMOS) INSTRUMENT IMAGED SATURN WITH HST AND REVEALED DRAMATIC DETAILS SEEN ONLY IN SPACE.

made by IR Labs is available to many visitors from the semiconductor industry.

The lab provides products and services to organizations such as universities, government agencies, and industrial laboratories, with about half its customers coming from outside the United States. Technology developed by Infrared Laboratories has been used on NASA's *Infrared Astronomical Satellite*, launched in 1983, and in the European Infrared Space Observatory.

Low heads the company of 30 full-time employees with vice presidents Steve Zoltowski and Elliott Solheid. The company is rooted in its technological and personnel relationship with the University of Arizona, often hiring students as temporary workers.

A member of the National Academy of Sciences since 1974, Low has been honored with awards ranging from the

Texas Instruments Foundation Special Founder's Prize in 1976 to the NASA Medal for Exceptional Scientific Achievement in 1984.

TECHNOLOGY AND INNOVATIONS

The infrared and cryogenic technology of IR Labs derives mainly from astronomy, but it is used in many other fields, such as the making of semiconductors. Infrared Laboratories offers the semiconductor industry a unique combination of low-temperature engineering, infrared optics and detectors, electronics, and software. In 1996, the lab introduced an infrared emission microscope, a critical tool for the semiconductor industry. These microscopes are based on a sensitive infrared camera developed at the University of Arizona for NASA's *Hubble Space Telescope*.

Many of the company's products and services are detailed at its Web site, www.irlabs.com. In the future, IR Labs will continue to develop, design, and build infrared and low-temperature instruments for the research community, and will continue to serve the semiconductor industry with even more powerful infrared microscopes.

"Infrared technology is helping in the design and manufacture of better computer chips, which helps bring down the cost of computers," Low says. "All this money we spend on scientific research has a direct payoff to our economy."

ACH YEAR, PIMA COMMUNITY COLLEGE (PCC) OPENS ITS DOORS TO MORE THAN 65,000 CREDIT AND NONCREDIT STUDENTS. SINCE THE FALL OF 1970, WHEN CLASSES WERE HELD IN AN AIRPORT HANGAR, THE COLLEGE HAS GROWN TO INCLUDE FIVE

campuses and more than 145 off-campus sites located throughout Tucson, Green Valley, Marana, and Nogales. "PCC has an open-door policy," says Chancellor Robert Jensen. "We welcome all who seek to increase their knowledge, gain skills, and enrich their lives."

Over the past 30 years, more than 400,000 people have enrolled at PCC, seeking everything from short-term training to two-year degrees. The fourth-largest multicampus community college in the nation, PCC currently offers more than 150 certificate and degree programs that can be completed in two years or less. Some certificates for direct employment can be completed in as little as two months. PCC offers approximately 30 university transfer programs, and most credits will transfer to Arizona's universities.

In addition, the college has strong technology programs, including archaeology, automotive, aviation, building construction, environmental studies, pharmacy, and semiconductor manufacturing. Some of PCC's newest offerings include public safety communications, computer programming, and auto collision repair. In addition, the college continues to offer programs in advanced technical fields and areas of high employability.

STUDENT SERVICES
PCC classes are small—Jensen says the average class size is 30—and the instructors are trained professionals dedicated to teaching. Arizona residents pay only $34 a credit hour, which means they can usually earn a college degree in two years or less for about $2,000 in tuition.

Students can choose classes from a variety of evening, weekend, short-term (eight weeks or less), and self-paced formats, while televised and Internet classes allow them to learn from home. In addition, PCC students have access to free academic and career counseling, tutoring, financial aid and veterans' assistance, basic skills assessment, disabled student resources, and other special programs. Libraries at four campuses house more than 250,000 books and multimedia items.

The intercollegiate athletic teams compete in men's baseball; women's

volleyball and softball; and men's and women's basketball, track, soccer, golf, cross-country, and tennis. Intramural and campus recreation programs are offered as well.

In addition, the college sponsors summer programs to help high school students get a jump on their college education, as well as explore new career options. At PCC, they can participate in regular credit courses for college or high school credit.

COMMUNITY IMPACT
PCC's impact reaches beyond its student population to benefit the Tucson

community and the business sector as well. For instance, PCC's Community Education Office offers hundreds of personal development courses and educational study tours throughout the Southwest and Mexico.

Students and area residents can enjoy music, dance, and multidisciplinary art at the PCC Center for the Arts (CFA). Located on the West Campus, the center's performance spaces are available on a rental basis for community performances and special events. The CFA Gallery hosts exhibitions of artwork by local, national, and international artists.

PCC offers customized degrees and on-site training to business and industry throughout Pima and Santa Cruz counties. A state-of-the-art computer-training center specializes in cost-effective training for employees, and is available for companies to conduct their own training. Free consulting services for business development, expansion, and retention are available for small businesses. The college can provide a company that is relocating to the Tucson area with a host of services and a custom-trained workforce.

"We are truly a major force in the economic development and well-being of Pima County," says Jensen.

THE FOURTH-LARGEST MULTICAMPUS COMMUNITY COLLEGE IN THE NATION, PIMA COMMUNITY COLLEGE (PCC) OPENS ITS DOORS TO MORE THAN 65,000 CREDIT AND NONCREDIT STUDENTS EACH YEAR (TOP).

PCC HAS STRONG TECHNOLOGY PROGRAMS, INCLUDING ARCHAEOLOGY, AUTOMOTIVE, AVIATION, BUILDING CONSTRUCTION, ENVIRONMENTAL STUDIES, PHARMACY, AND SEMICONDUCTOR MANUFACTURING, AND CONTINUES TO OFFER PROGRAMS IN ADVANCED TECHNICAL FIELDS AND AREAS OF HIGH EMPLOYABILITY (BOTTOM).

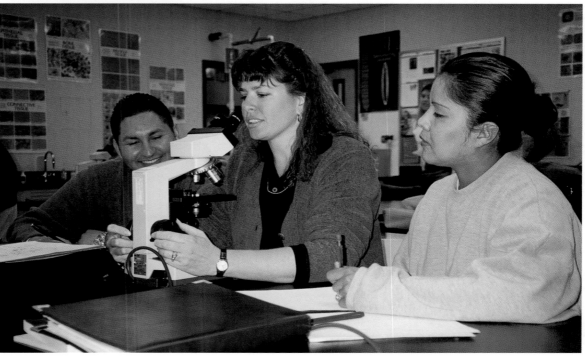

HEN THE UNIVERSITY OF ARIZONA (UA) COLLEGE OF MEDICINE OPENED ITS DOORS IN 1967 WITH JUST 32 MEDICAL STUDENTS AND 21 FACULTY MEMBERS, FEW COULD HAVE IMAGINED IT WOULD EVOLVE INTO a thriving academic health sciences center.

But, in a little more than three decades, the Arizona Health Sciences Center (AHSC) is setting new standards for health care education, research, patient care, and service throughout the state and beyond. AHSC has grown to include some 2,000 students, 5,000 employees, and 1,000 faculty members.

The Arizona Health Sciences Center has an annual budget of more than $500 million, but only 10 percent comes from state tax dollars. The support of the people of Arizona translates into an $8 million to $12 million increase in the endowment fund each year.

These figures illustrate the dollar impact the center has made on the community, but there are other, more intangible benefits that the Arizona Health Sciences Center provides. "Our research efforts have a major impact. We bring in a tremendous number of grants, and there are many spin-off companies that are related to our biotechnology research," explains Dr. James E. Dalen, vice president for health sciences and dean of the College of Medicine. "In addition, 90 per-cent of our employees, and their wives or husbands, are college graduates. They are very interested and involved in the community, the schools, and the arts."

THE COLLEGES

The Arizona Health Sciences Center includes the UA Colleges of Medicine, Nursing, and Pharmacy, and the School of Health Professions, as well as University Medical Center. The center's pharmacy program is ranked among the top five in the nation, while the nursing program is ranked in the top 10. University Medical Center is among the nation's best hospitals for cardiac care, according to *U.S. News & World Report*'s annual guide to America's best hospitals.

Four hundred medical students are enrolled in the College of Medicine, and another 400 resident physicians receive training at the college in a variety of medical specialties. More than 2,200 students have earned degrees from the College of Medicine.

AHSC has 11 Centers of Excellence dedicated to specific areas of research, clinical care, and teaching. The Arizona Cancer Center is renowned for its research discoveries and compassionate patient care. Its internationally recognized medical professionals and scientists study how cancer starts, how to improve treatments, and what can be done to prevent it. The UA Sarver Heart Center conducts more than 90 percent of cardiovascular research in Arizona, including use of the artificial heart, while the Respiratory Sciences Center has become a leading source of research to better understand and treat asthma, emphysema, and other respiratory diseases. The Arizona Poison and Drug Information Center answers more than 70,000 calls a year regarding bites, stings, household chemicals, and more.

The Steele Memorial Children's Research Center is the state's only research center dedicated to children's health, while the Arizona Prevention Center forges partnerships with communities throughout the state to promote health and develop prevention strategies. The Arizona Arthritis Center is dedicated to biomedical research into the causes and treatments of more than 100 forms of arthritis. And the Center for Toxicology plays a crucial role in the

▶ ROBIN STANCLIFF

UNIVERSITY MEDICAL CENTER AT THE ARIZONA HEALTH SCIENCES CENTER IS THE PRIMARY TEACHING HOSPITAL FOR THE UNIVERSITY OF ARIZONA COLLEGE OF MEDICINE. THE HOSPITAL IS CONSISTENTLY RANKED AMONG THE NATION'S BEST FOR CARDIAC AND CANCER CARE.

EXCELLENT PATIENT CARE, TEACHING, RESEARCH, AND COMMUNITY SERVICE ARE THE FOUR HALLMARKS OF THE ARIZONA HEALTH SCIENCES CENTER. THE PERSONAL TOUCH OF PHYSICIANS LIKE MICHAEL GRAHAM, M.D., IS A REMINDER THAT ACADEMIC MEDICINE IS NOT NECESSARILY ACADEMIC.

cleanup of the nation's hazardous waste sites. Other facilities include the Center for Health Outcomes and Pharmaco Economic Research, which is seeking lower costs for medications; the Arizona Emergency Medicine Research Center, which is committed to improving emergency services and medical training, education, and research; and the Arizona Center on Aging, which brings together members of many campus departments and community leaders to address topics critical to aging.

"The centers are multidisciplinary," says Dalen. "The Arizona Cancer Center has faculty from many departments in the university. It's one of the most prominent cancer centers in the country. And there's a long-standing relationship between radiology and optical sciences. They exchange research and developments. It's one of the remarkable things about the UA, and I think that's one of our greatest strengths."

A RESEARCH CENTER

The Arizona Health Sciences Center attracts more than $85 million in research grants and gifts each year, and is consistently ranked among the top U.S. public and private research institutions. Researchers are working on a range of basic, clinical,

and applied research projects to help combat diseases like cancer, heart disease, asthma, arthritis, and many others.

University Medical Center (UMC), a 365-bed, private, nonprofit facility, opened in 1971, and provides primary care as well as advanced treatment on an inpatient and outpatient basis in more than 70 specialty areas. The state's first heart transplant was performed at UMC in 1979, and since then, the hospital has become the region's only comprehensive transplant center, boasting some of the best long-term survival rates for heart transplant patients in the world.

GIVING BACK TO ARIZONA

The Arizona Health Sciences Center reaches out to communities throughout the state in many ways. For example, the Arizona Telemedicine Program allows AHSC specialists to provide medical consultation, using high-resolution video imaging and other technology, to rural physicians and other health professionals to improve patients' lives.

Through the Rural Health Professions Program, medicine, nursing, pharmacy, and nurse practitioner students receive part of their education at rural sites nationwide—with the goal that they will consider practicing in rural commu-

nities. Further, the UA Rural Health Office Mobile Clinic provides primary medical care services for moderate- to low-income and underserved populations in three southern Arizona communities. And the Arizona Arthritis Center, the UA Sarver Center, and the Steele Memorial Children's Research Center reach out to Arizona's Native American reservations, conducting outreach clinics and other activities.

The AHSC Phoenix Campus was established in 1994 to meet the needs of medical students in Maricopa County and to provide education and community outreach to the area. About a third of UA's third- and fourth-year medical students complete medical school there, participating in clinical rotations at teaching hospitals in the Valley.

The Arizona Health Sciences Center is currently planning its newest school, the College of Public Health, which will study the health of populations, with a focus on preventive health care.

For more than three decades, the Arizona Health Sciences Center has continued to grow and evolve to meet the needs of the region. Proud of its contributions to the community and its high standing in the health care field, the center is an integral part of the Tucson landscape.

I N A COMMUNITY BLESSED WITH RUGGED, COLORFUL LANDSCAPES AND A HERITAGE RICH WITH HISPANIC AND NATIVE AMERICAN INFLUENCES, SEAVER FRANKS ARCHITECTS, INC., A.I.A., IN 2000 CELEBRATED ITS 25TH ANNIVERSARY OF CREATING ARCHITECTURE THAT RESPECTS—

and reflects—Tucson's intriguing history, delicate environment, and unique architectural style.

"At Seaver Franks Architects, we're dedicated to the continued pursuit of design excellence, with an emphasis in regional architectural solutions that make sense in the high Sonoran Desert," says Michael W. Franks, managing partner. "We continue to explore ways to be more responsive to our environment and sensitive to the community for which we are designing. In the desert, environmental factors such as intense heat and light need to be considered along with each client's individual needs."

BLENDING TRADITIONAL AND CONTEMPORARY

Founded in 1975 by Douglas L. Seaver, the company quickly established a reputation for designing specialty facilities exclusively for private sector clients. Seaver, who had worked in the offices of Chicago's internationally influential architect Ludwig Mies van der Rohe, established the firm by drawing on his experience in technically efficient and sophisticated architecture.

Franks, a Tucson native, joined the firm in 1981, bringing with him a long-standing family tradition of awareness and respect for regional style. For decades, his father designed and built custom residences in the Santa Catalina foothills as a co-owner of La Quinta Homes. In addition to the two principals, each architect within the firm contributes his or her own expertise and diversity, allowing the Seaver Franks design philosophy to continually evolve.

"Our style blends traditional architectural elements of form, texture, and color with contemporary influences that technology and experience teach us," says Franks, who is responsible for client development, overall project management, and design team supervision. "We as architects have the responsibility of interpreting these influences and incorporating them into our architectural environment."

Together, this team has completed hundreds of projects around the United States, encompassing in excess of 2.5 million square feet with a construction value of more than $3 billion. The projects include corporate offices, master-planned

AMONG SEAVER FRANKS ARCHITECTS, INC., A.I.A.'S MOST NOTABLE ACCOMPLISHMENTS ARE (CLOCKWISE FROM TOP) THE WESTIN LA PALOMA IN TUCSON, THE DE CONCINI LAW OFFICES, AND THE CANYON PASS AT DOVE MOUNTAIN CONTROLLED ACCESS STRUCTURE.

JAMES YOCHUM PHOTOGRAPHY

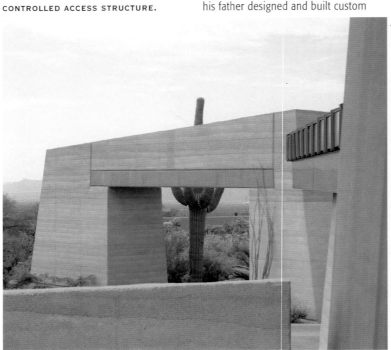

JAMES BRETT

JAMES YOCHUM PHOTOGRAPHY

communities, hotels, country clubs, churches, restaurants, casinos, and luxury residences. Although Seaver Franks has also worked with clients on projects in other parts of the world, most of its work is done in Tucson, and many of its clients are repeat clients. The firm and its associate architects are proud of their reputation for regionally responsive architecture, and they enjoy sharing this design philosophy with their clients.

For private residences, each project is site-specific and responsive to its surroundings—both natural and man-made. During the design process, the Seaver Franks architects strive to create a home that is personal and unique to the client's lifestyle, and one that is reflective of the site's and region's distinctive characteristics.

SHAPING THE TUCSON SKYLINE

Among the firm's most outstanding accomplishments is the Tucson Westin La Paloma Resort, designed in 1982. With stone arches, long breezeways, and terracotta tile roofs, the resort is reminiscent of a traditional territorial hacienda. "Although Tucson was home to many beautiful dude ranches and lodges, La Paloma was one of the area's first modern destination resorts," says Seaver. With convention facilities, luxury guest suites, and a variety of dining choices, it set a new standard for Tucson.

The firm is equally proud of the De Concini Law Offices, a project that blended traditional and contemporary forms and materials. Featuring modern steel and glass construction, combined with a massive stone arcade, the striking

office complex is punctuated by cast stone murals that tell a story of the Sonoran Desert. According to Seaver, it was inspired in part by downtown Tucson's historic St. Augustine Cathedral.

Seaver Franks has also designed several notable churches in Tucson, Scottsdale, and New Mexico. "Our goal is to reflect a church's spiritual identity in architectural form, heightening the worship experience through integration of space, light, and materials," says Seaver. A prime example of this philosophy is St. Thomas the Apostle Catholic Church in Tucson. Nestled at the foot of the Santa Catalina Mountains, the church blends modern and traditional southwestern elements in a bright, open design.

Seaver Franks received an Excellence in Architecture Merit award from the Arizona Society of the American Institute of Architects for its St. Thomas the Apostle design. The firm has been honored with numerous other design awards throughout the years, including a Gold Nugget award from Pacific Coast Builders, the Outstanding Architect award from the American Subcontractors Association, the Office Building of the Year award, the Excellence in Architectural Design award, and the Building of the Year award from *Metal Construction News*.

Other noteworthy Seaver Franks projects in the Tucson area include the La Paloma Country Club, La Paloma Corporate Center, Wilmot Corporate Center, Oro Valley Police Headquarters, Tucson Savings and Loan, and numerous luxury residences in the Catalina foothills and Tortolita Mountains.

Over the years, Seaver Franks has discovered that Tucson presents an ideal forum for an evolving architectural practice. Although the area continues to experience rapid growth, its residents remain committed to preserving its unique, southwestern lifestyle. For architects who have built a thriving business by staying in tune with this lifestyle, design opportunities and the challenge to create responsible regional architecture are rewarding.

"We are privileged to have been able to help shape the Tucson fabric and create environments where our clients live, work, worship, and play," says Franks. "Our work is touching all parts of the community at many levels, and we feel this is something that truly sets us apart from our peers."

THE FIRM STRIVES TO CREATE UNIQUE DESIGN SOLUTIONS—SUCH AS (CLOCKWISE FROM TOP LEFT) A PRIVATE RESIDENCE IN THE CANYONS AT FINGER ROCK NEIGHBORHOOD, THE CANYON PASS AT DOVE MOUNTAIN SALES AND INFORMATION CENTER, AND THE ST. THOMAS THE APOSTLE PARISH CHURCH—THAT RESPECT AND REFLECT TUSCON'S INTRIGUING HISTORY, DELICATE ENVIRONMENT, AND UNIQUE ARCHITECTURAL STYLE.

1976 - 1986

GLOBAL ATMOSPHERICS, INC.	1976	THE LODGE AT VENTANA CANYON	1984
IBM	1978	TRACER RESEARCH CORPORATION	1984
PASCUA YAQUI TRIBE OF ARIZONA/		U S WEST	1984
CASINO OF THE SUN	1978	HONEYWELL INTERNATIONAL INC.	1985
SUNQUEST INFORMATION SYSTEMS, INC.	1979	VENTANA MEDICAL SYSTEMS, INC.	1985
5 STAR TERMITE AND PEST CONTROL	1980	GROMATZKY DUPREE AND ASSOCIATES	
GEO ADVERTISING AND MARKETING	1981	SOUTHWEST LLC	1986
SWS ELECTRONICS & COMPUTERS	1982	THE WESTIN LA PALOMA	1986
NORTHWEST MEDICAL CENTER	1983		

REACHING TEMPERATURES FOUR OR FIVE TIMES GREATER THAN THAT OF THE SUN, LIGHTNING STRIKES THE EARTH UP TO 100 TIMES EVERY SECOND. IT KILLS MORE PEOPLE YEARLY THAN ANY OTHER SINGLE METEOROLOGICAL PHENOMENON. "IT'S LIKE A

wild animal," says Patrick J. Zumbusch, president of Global Atmospherics, Inc. "It's a beautiful animal, but very dangerous."

Established in Tucson in 1976, Global Atmospherics, Inc. (GAI) is charged with a specific mission—the tracking of lightning. The company designs lightning detection systems for a variety of applications around the world and maintains a continentwide network of lightning detectors in the United States. It is the world's largest manufacturer and system integrator of lightning detection and location equipment and services in the world, with products in more than 30 countries. These devices range from more simplified, single-sensor devices used to monitor local and regional lightning phenomena to sophisticated national networks that measure a wide range of lightning parameters.

GAI's customers call on the company for a variety of needs. "The electric utility clients want to know when lightning hits their line," Zumbusch says. "That means

THE U.S. AIR FORCE DEPENDS ON REAL-TIME LIGHTNING DATA TO EVALUATE WEATHER CONDITIONS PRIOR TO LAUNCHES (TOP).

GLOBAL ATMOSPHERICS, INC.'S (GAI) NETWORK CONTROL CENTER IN TUCSON (BOTTOM).

electricity is running amok on a system." Global Atmospherics also searches power lines for design weaknesses. "In a different application, golf courses want to protect patrons, and businesses want an uninterrupted operating environment. Lightning is a reoccurring problem for a host of customers, and that's where we come in," says Zumbusch.

SUPPLIER OF LIGHTNING INFORMATION

Started in conjunction with the Electric Power Research Institute (EPRI), Global Atmospherics also owns and operates the National Lightning Detection Network™ (NLDN), which provides lightning data to customers like the Federal Aviation Administration (FAA), National Weather Service (NWS), Department of Defense, and numerous industrial companies. In fact, 40 of the top 60 electric power companies in the United States use GAI's services, as do many of their respective Fortune 500 clients.

The NLDN consists of more than 100 remote, ground-based sensing stations that monitor lightning activity across the continental United States. The sensors differentiate lightning strikes from the atmosphere's vast amount of background noise. Within seconds of a lightning strike, Global Atmospherics processes the information via a satellite-based communications network to derive the exact location, time, polarity, and peak amplitude of each strike. Pinpointing lightning strikes lets clients know if a storm is coming and whether precautionary actions should be taken.

Global Atmospherics supplies this data to businesses and agencies across the nation, including Fidelity; Charles Schwab; Universal Studios; American Express; America Online; most of the large insurance firms, including CNA and State Farm; airlines such as United, American, and Northwest; and telecom-

munications companies like Bell Atlantic, AT&T, and MCI. GAI also supplies lightning data to the NWS' storm tracking system. The FAA uses the company's information to direct aircraft, while the U.S. Forest Service uses it to identify possible sources of forest fires. In fact, Global Atmospherics is the only private entity providing national weather information to the U.S. government.

Lightning damage to individuals is also a major concern to Global Atmospherics, and the company is now devising ways to help protect people against lightning. It currently posts a lightning safety page on its Web site—www.glatmos.com—and will begin offering tailored personal warnings in the near future. Its goal is to let people know when they need to get off the phone, get their kids out of the pool, or back up computer documents. Another goal is to eventually devise ways to automatically protect household appliances against lightning-induced power surges. "I'd really like to serve each resident across the country, those people who may be remote but could still benefit from a smart severe weather system," Zumbusch says.

SCIENCE AND BUSINESS

The foundation of Global Atmospherics was laid in the mid-1970s, when University of Arizona scientists Drs. E. Philip Krider, Burt Pifer, and Martin Uman were researching the properties and behavior of lightning. Their work centered on the use of magnetic direction-finding technology to locate electromagnetic signals produced by lightning.

Searching for ways to prevent forest fires in Alaska, the Bureau of Land Management commissioned the scientists to create a sensor that could detect and locate far-off lightning strikes. The project led to the formation of Lightning Location and Protection in 1976, which introduced the first location system capable of automatically locating cloud-to-ground lightning over large areas. "Now, with microprocessors pervasive in our everyday lives, the vulnerable areas are in our electronics and there is hardly anyone immune from a power disruption," says Zumbusch.

According to Zumbusch, Global Atmospherics spends two to three times more on research and development than the average high-tech company. The company is driven by a curiosity about lightning phenomenology, as well as its practical applications. "Although we are measuring Mother Nature's energy—her kinetic pulse, so to speak—there's still very little we know. We need to become much more intelligent about what she is trying to tell us," says Zumbusch.

The company maintains an academic tie to the University of Arizona, conducting research projects with UA and other universities around the world. "Notwithstanding these ties and developed expertise, our true strength lies with our employees. Their creativity and commitment stand second to none," Zumbusch states.

Global Atmospherics is proud to be a part of Tucson. The company is strategically located and has ready access to its clients across the globe. Adds Zumbusch, "We want to be part of a good environment and community. Tucson reflects those traits."

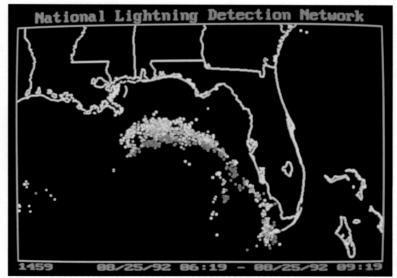

FOR MORE THAN 40 YEARS, IBM HAS BEEN THE LEADER IN PROVIDING CUSTOMERS WORLDWIDE WITH SOLUTIONS TO THEIR INFORMATION STORAGE NEEDS. IBM VIRTUALLY CREATED THE INFORMATION STORAGE INDUSTRY IN 1952 WHEN

its engineers invented the components that enable mechanical tape buffering. The company's half-inch tape reel, introduced soon thereafter, set the industry standard for the next 20 years. In 1956, IBM created the first hard disk drive based on the principle of storing data magnetically on a spinning disk.

Since those first successes, IBM's Storage Subsystems Division (SSD) has developed and brought to market countless innovations in storage hardware systems, storage management software, and storage components. SSD is truly a global operation with development and manufacturing operations around the world. The mission of the Tucson site, which plays a key role in IBM's storage

strategy and objectives, is to provide the research and development of advanced storage and retrieval products for workstations and for mid-range and high-end computer systems.

"Storage is a very important opportunity to serve our customers," says Richard T. Myers Jr., site general manager. "With the explosion of information, storage is more important now than ever."

IBM TUCSON

Some of the products developed at the IBM Tucson site, which employs approximately 1,300 people, include magnetic tape subsystems, automated tape libraries, optical storage subsystems and libraries, disk storage controllers,

and related storage management software. IBM remains poised to drive the information storage industry with breakthrough technology and marketing innovations that push storage capacities, capabilities, and customer satisfaction to new levels.

"IBM Tucson is a very vibrant and technical site," says Myers. "Our customers depend on the storage products we develop. The volume of information is growing exponentially, fueled by the growth of e-business and Internet applications. When you go on the Internet, all the information you see out there has to be stored and retrieved quickly. It's our job to develop robust storage devices and software to help our customers efficiently manage their data."

The IBM 7133 Serial Disk System, introduced in 1995, was the first storage subsystem to implement Serial Storage Architecture, a new industry standard for high-performance, low-cost, reliable

INTRODUCED IN 1995, THE IBM 7133 SERIAL DISK SYSTEM (LEFT) WAS THE FIRST STORAGE SUBSYSTEM TO IMPLEMENT SERIAL STORAGE ARCHITECTURE, A NEW INDUSTRY STANDARD FOR HIGH-PERFORMANCE, LOW-COST, RELIABLE TRANSFER OF DATA.

ONE OF THE PRODUCTS DEVELOPED AT THE IBM TUCSON SITE IS THE MAGSTAR 3590 TAPE SUBSYSTEM (FRONT VIEW, TOP RIGHT; REAR VIEW, BOTTOM RIGHT).

transfer of data. The system launched IBM's mission of providing robust enterprise storage solutions for the open marketplace. Today, these systems support a wide range of Unix and PC servers, including those from Sun Microsystems and Hewlett-Packard, among others.

In addition to developing leading-edge storage hardware and software solutions for IBM's customers and original equipment manufacturer (OEM) partners, the company and its employees continually strive to maintain a close partnership with the local community through volunteer activities and contributions. Over the years, IBM has had a long tradition of working with local government agencies and organizations in support of education, community programs, and the arts in the Tucson area.

Located in a technical park owned by the University of Arizona (UA), IBM cooperates with the school on research projects, and partners with the graduate business school. Through IBM's co-op program, about 125 interns—mostly UA students—worked at the site in summer 1999.

MAKING THE COMMUNITY A BETTER PLACE TO LIVE

IBM Tucson strives to be more than just a business enterprise to its home community. The company has three key programs that help employees, retirees, and their spouses support community activities. They are the Fund for Community Service; the IBM Matching Grants Program for Higher Education, Hospitals, and the Arts; and the IBM K-12 Matching Grants Program.

Since the start of its operations in Tucson in 1979, IBM and its employees have also donated more than $10 million to the United Way of Greater Tucson, and have the highest annual average gift and per capita contributions to the United Way compared with all other IBM sites in the country. In addition, IBM Tucson employees lead the company in the number of volunteers who participate in community and charity events.

IBM also holds an annual Day of Caring, in which employees get time off to pitch in on projects around Tucson. In a recent project, employees helped renovate a shelter for battered women, assisting more than a dozen other agencies. "There's pride in technical accomplishment, as well as in what we do in the community," Myers says. "At IBM, we're especially proud of our role in making the Tucson community a better place for everyone to live."

THE MISSION OF THE TUCSON SITE, WHICH PLAYS A KEY ROLE IN IBM'S STORAGE STRATEGY AND OBJECTIVES, IS TO PROVIDE THE RESEARCH AND DEVELOPMENT OF ADVANCED STORAGE AND RETRIEVAL PRODUCTS, SUCH AS THE IBM 3490 MODEL F00 TAPE SUBSYSTEM (TOP LEFT) AND THE IBM MAGSTAR VIRTUAL TAPE SERVER (TOP RIGHT).

IBM'S STORAGE SUBSYSTEMS DIVISION REMAINS POISED TO DRIVE THE INFORMATION STORAGE INDUSTRY WITH BREAKTHROUGH TECHNOLOGY AND MARKETING INNOVATIONS, SUCH AS THE IBM ENTERPRISE STORAGE SERVER, ALSO KNOWN AS SHARK (BOTTOM).

FROM THEIR FIRST ENCOUNTER WITH SPANISH INVADERS NEARLY 500 YEARS AGO, YAQUIS HAVE HELD TENACIOUSLY TO THEIR WAY OF LIFE. AS JESUIT PRIESTS WORKED TO CONVERT THE TRIBE TO CATHOLICISM, YAQUI ELDERS DEMANDED THAT MANY

aspects of their centuries-old beliefs, including their sacred Deer Dancer, blend with the new religion. The result of centuries of careful preservation by tribal elders is seen in the rich, complex, and unique religious ceremonies of the Pascua Yaqui Tribe of Arizona.

"From a cultural standpoint, we are one of the few tribes still maintaining our traditions," says Fernando Escalante, Ph.D., vice chairman of the tribe. He credits the determination of tribal elders with maintaining the Yaqui culture during the introduction of Christianity and the tumultuous centuries that followed.

These hardy descendants of the ancient Uto-Aztecans intermittently fought the Spanish and then the Mexicans, gaining a reputation as fierce, independent warriors and skilled battle tacticians. But they eventually faced intense persecution, imprisonment, and deportation from their beloved Rio Yaqui to other areas of Mexico. The Mexican military occupied Yaqui country until as late as the 1970s. Numerous Yaquis migrated north in the late 1800s, many as employees of the Southern Pacific Railroad. They created communities near

Tucson and Phoenix, and four communities in and around Tucson, including the reservation, and a fifth at Guadalupe, a suburb of Phoenix, thrive today.

While Yaquis began settling in the United States in the 1880s, it wasn't until 1964 that the tribe was granted 202 acres southwest of Tucson through the legislative efforts of U.S. Representative Morris K. Udall. But federal recognition as a tribe didn't come until September 18, 1978. The tribe celebrates Recognition Day every year on that day, starting with mass in the morning and a variety of activities for adults and children throughout the day.

The reservation now has 1,150 acres and owns several thousand acres that are not part of the reservation. About one-third of the tribe's 12,500 members live on the reservation. The tribe elects 11 council members every four years, and from among its members, the council elects a chairman, vice chairman, secretary, and treasurer.

Much of the tribe's progress has been financed by revenues from the Casino of the Sun, launched in 1994, after the tribe signed a gaming compact with the state. The forerunner of the casino

was a bingo hall opened in the early 1980s. At that time, the Pascua Yaqui Tribe was one of only four tribes in Arizona to sign a gaming compact with the state to operate a bingo hall.

TRIBAL EMPLOYERS

Tribal government is the largest employer on the reservation, with about 1,000 employees. The Casino of the Sun, which employs 700—about 80 percent tribal members—offers 500 slot machines featuring nickel, quarter, dollar, and five-dollar play; video poker; video blackjack; and bingo in the casino's Bingo Dome. Visitors can enjoy the casino's all-you-can-eat buffet with prime rib served daily. Weekly half-off prices and food specials are featured. Free shuttle service to and from the Casino of the Sun is offered daily at several locations throughout Tucson.

Revenues generated by the Casino of the Sun have allowed the Pascua Yaqui Tribe to make vast improvements on the reservation, including construction of a state-of-the-art health clinic, which includes a dialysis facility. "We fund our police and fire departments, plus various other programs we have,

TODAY, THE PASCUA YAQUI TRIBE OF ARIZONA RESERVATION HAS 1,150 ACRES, WHERE ABOUT ONE-THIRD OF THE TRIBE'S 12,500 MEMBERS LIVE. THE TRIBE ELECTS 11 COUNCIL MEMBERS EVERY FOUR YEARS, AND FROM AMONG ITS MEMBERS, THE COUNCIL ELECTS A CHAIRMAN, VICE CHAIRMAN, SECRETARY, AND TREASURER.

▲ MARTHA LOCKERT PHOTOGRAPHY

THE TRIBE'S LARGEST BUSINESS ENTER-
PRISE, THE CASINO OF THE SUN, HAS
SOME 700 EMPLOYEES, ABOUT 80 PER-
CENT OF WHOM ARE TRIBAL MEMBERS.
IT OFFERS 500 SLOT MACHINES FEATUR-
ING NICKEL, QUARTER, DOLLAR, AND
FIVE-DOLLAR PLAY; VIDEO POKER; VIDEO
BLACKJACK; AND BINGO IN THE CASINO'S
BINGO DOME, AS WELL AS TRANSPOR-
TATION TO AND FROM THE CASINO.

such as health, education, social services, vocational training, and housing," says Escalante. The fire department has grown to 24 members and the police force numbers 27. Both departments have up-to-date equipment, and the reservation is served by the 911 emergency call-in service.

During the past five years, more than 500 jobs have been created, more than 180 new homes have been built, and the tribe has provided $1 million a year for education overall. The casino ranks high among area businesses, putting millions of dollars a year into the local economy through purchases from vendors. Escalante and other tribal leaders see education as the key to a bright future for the tribe. "We want a highly educated tribe," he states. "Every member who wants an education should have one." The Pascua Yaqui Tribe set aside $1.3 million for scholarships in 1999.

Besides the casino, the tribe also operates the Pascua Yaqui Adobe Company, which manufactures and sells adobe brick for housing and commercial structures, and the Yaqui Artisans and Smoke Shop, which sells gift items and tobacco products. The casino is the primary means to generate revenues that can be invested in developing additional businesses, say tribal executives. The tribe has a program to fund tribal members' small-business ventures and Escalante and other leaders envision a time of economic self-sufficiency. "We do not want

THE RESERVATION'S HEALTH FACILITY
WELCOMES PATIENTS WITH A SIGN IN
YOEME, THE YAQUI LANGUAGE, THAT
READS YAQUI HEALING HOUSE.

to rely on the federal government. We want to provide for ourselves."

LIVING LEGACY

As proof of a thriving Yaqui culture, tribal members speak some Yoeme, the original Yaqui language that is used in many traditional ceremonies, and Yoeme classes are taught on the reservation. Most tribal members speak English and Spanish fluently, and maintain a close relationship with Yaquis in Mexico.

The internationally known Deer Dancer is a focal point of most Yaqui religious ceremonies in rites that blend ancient traditions with Christianity. *Pascua* in Spanish means "Easter," and the Pascua Yaqui are world famous for their Easter celebrations. The Deer Dancer, a major participant in the tribe's Palm Sunday

ceremonies, originates from a spiritual realm of bright, beautiful flowers that are empowered to destroy evil and bring out goodness. This revered symbol of good is used in the tribal logo. Easter observances begin on Ash Wednesday and continue each week through Lent, a time of intense prayer and sacrifice for tribal members and the end of the Yaqui year. Respectful visitors are welcomed to the ceremonies. Out of esteem for tribal members, the casino is closed during Holy Week.

Escalante says that the Easter celebrations are an important element in preserving Yaqui culture—a time for tribal leaders to remind the tribe of the need to carry on ancient traditions and to honor hundreds of years of a proud, vibrant heritage.

FOR HEALTH CARE COMPANIES WITH COMPLEX CLINICAL AND ADMINISTRATIVE INFORMATION TO MANAGE, CHANCES ARE SUNQUEST INFORMATION SYSTEMS, INC. HAS A SOLUTION. SINCE 1979, SUNQUEST HAS IMPROVED PATIENT CARE through its innovative information systems and service excellence.

The company designs, develops, sells, and supports a wide range of clinical information systems that streamline the operations of everything from individual departments within small hospitals to large, multi-facility health care networks. Whatever a health care organization's size, Sunquest systems create work-flow efficiencies, reduce errors, alert health care professionals to clinical events, and disseminate clinical and administrative information throughout an integrated delivery network, thus improving profitability.

Headquartered in Tucson, Sunquest employs more than 800 people locally, as well as in Johnstown, Plano, Salt Lake City, and the United Kingdom. The company has installed systems in approximately 1,200 health care sites worldwide.

A WIDE RANGE OF PRODUCTS

Sunquest is dedicated to providing information solutions that meet the user's functional and operational needs. Products include laboratory, diagnostic imaging, and pharmacy information systems. The company also markets the Clinical Event Manager alert system, while its consulting division, Balanced View Consulting, supports customers throughout the installation process.

Sunquest's Laboratory Information System is a comprehensive, high-speed product with clinical and management capabilities for hospital, reference, commercial, and regional laboratories. The software can be customized by adding modules that allow multifacility processing and outreach. Supporting modules within the system provide for requisition entry and enhanced reporting. Sunquest's Lab Data Network connects geographically dispersed laboratories across a health care network, helping organizations reduce operating costs and maximize resources.

Sunquest's Radiology Information System improves day-to-day operations within the radiology environment. Users can process more patients, measure staff and equipment utilization, and improve service to the clinician community. Other features include patient scheduling and monitoring, film management, enhanced management reporting, diagnostic reporting and optional mammography

tracking, inventory control, and image viewing.

Sunquest's Pharmacy Information System merges inpatient and outpatient records for improved medication management. It offers drug intervention checking and monitoring, and a system inventory component that helps pharmacists keep track of inventory.

Clinical Event Manager, Sunquest's communications system, uses state-of-the-art technology to monitor patient care and alert health care providers of significant patient events via E-mail or pager. The unit is small enough to wear on the waist or slip in a shirt pocket.

Sunquest professionals are trained to provide high-quality client support. During the installation process, they document, train, and support hospital personnel to ensure a smooth and successful transition. Sunquest's Tucson and Johnstown sites even house facilities to train clients in-house. By developing superior products, installing them quickly and efficiently, and providing ongoing support, Sunquest makes sure clients continue to benefit from their investments.

STRONG COMMERCIAL LABORATORY DIVISION

Sunquest's commercial laboratory division, Antrim Corporation, was founded in 1982. This division provides lab management solutions for large and small reference laboratories, as well as hospi-

SIDNEY GOLDBLATT COFOUNDED SUNQUEST INFORMATION SYSTEMS, INC. IN 1979, AND CURRENTLY SERVES AS CEO (TOP).

HEADQUARTERED IN TUCSON, SUNQUEST EMPLOYS MORE THAN 800 PEOPLE LOCALLY, AND IS DEDICATED TO PROVIDING INFORMATION SOLUTIONS THAT MEET THE USER'S FUNCTIONAL AND OPERATIONAL NEEDS (BOTTOM).

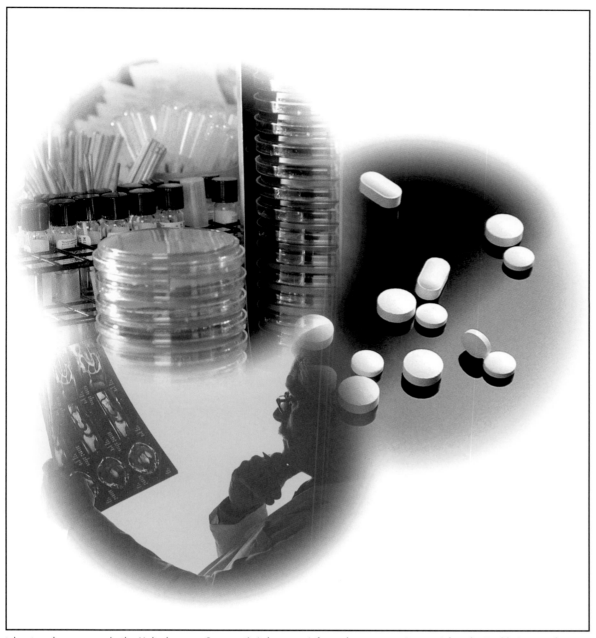

tal outreach programs, in the United States, Canada, Mexico, and the United Kingdom.

Laboratory information systems designed by Antrim support all aspects of laboratory operations—testing and materials management, billing, and accounts receivable and payable. Antrim aims to respond to the ever changing health care environment and streamline day-to-day operations within the laboratory, while providing ongoing quality service.

Antrim also develops Answers Medical Information Systems for the commercial and medical reference laboratory marketplace. Modules within the system provide order entry, tracking and report generation, work lists, and results reporting.

WORLDWIDE PRESENCE

More than 1,200 sites around the world use Sunquest systems. For instance,

Sunquest's Laboratory Information System is used by Capital Health Authority of Edmonton, Alberta; St. Mary's Hospital in Norton, Virginia; and Catholic Healthcare West, a 35-hospital group headquartered in San Francisco. In addition, California-based hospital system Sutter Health uses Sunquest's Radiology Information System, while doctors at University of Utah Hospital and Clinics receive urgent messages with Clinical Event Manager.

Most recently, Sunquest contracted with Adventist Health System, one of the country's largest integrated health care delivery systems, to provide a laboratory system and consulting support to standardize laboratory processes across the network's 14 hospitals.

"When we looked at information systems, we found Sunquest shared our emphasis on bottom-line results through a singular solution," says Hal

Lexow, Adventist Health System vice president of information services and multistate hospital division chief information officer. "Our hospitals vary greatly in their levels of sophistication. Sunquest's product is so robust it can satisfy multiple needs: large facilities benefit from more advanced features, while smaller hospitals gain solutions they could never realize on their own."

"Our Laboratory Information System is perfect for a health care system like Adventist," says Sunquest Chief Operating Officer Mark Emkjer. "The product is highly modular—big enough to encompass a comprehensive network, while small enough to accommodate singular needs. Adventist is building an informational foundation that will serve them well into the future. These are the types of partnerships we're in business to build."

FROM A ONE-PERSON, ONE-TRUCK OPERATION IN 1980, 5 STAR TERMITE AND PEST CONTROL, INC.—FOUNDED BY SHELBY HAWKINS—HAS GROWN INTO A COMPANY WITH 16 EMPLOYEES, NINE TRUCKS, AND A GROSS INCOME IN 1998 OF MORE THAN

$1 million. Pest control was a natural marriage of Hawkins' many interests. With degrees in social science and recreation, as well as interests in chemistry, geology, entomology, and natural healing, Hawkins—a Brigham Young University graduate—believes that pest control combines all of these things, which definitely keeps her from getting bored. "I believe that learning is a continuous process," she says. "When we stop learning, we are dead."

Hawkins started 5 Star Termite and Pest Control on February 8, 1980. She began inspecting structures for termites while continuing employment as a social worker. Later that same year, she received her state inspection license and quit social

work to devote more time to the pest control work. Raising three small children while trying to get a new business going was becoming a drain on her energy as well as on her bank account. She was offered a position with a chemical company in Salt Lake City and was about to accept it when a contract for $15,000 was offered to 5 Star. "Money was a real motivator to me then, and still is," Hawkins says. "After that first large contract, my business began to increase dramatically."

In the beginning, Hawkins worked out of her home, often putting in six-day workweeks and frequently carting her young children with her to early morning appointments. She learned how to fix

her own truck, operate and fix the tools of her trade, and market her business. As the business warranted, she gradually added employees, trucks, and equipment.

Hawkins has become known as a pioneer in the pest control industry. She was the first woman termite inspector in the state of Arizona and the first woman to obtain a license in the state for a pest control company. Many of her customers, male and female, choose 5 Star because they feel very comfortable dealing with a woman.

SOUTH PACIFIC CONNECTION
Hawkins came close to selling 5 Star after the chemical chlordane was taken off the

WITH DEGREES IN SOCIAL SCIENCE AND RECREATION, AS WELL AS INTERESTS IN CHEMISTRY, GEOLOGY, ENTOMOLOGY, AND NATURAL HEALING, SHELBY HAWKINS, FOUNDER OF 5 STAR TERMITE AND PEST CONTROL, INC., BELIEVES THAT PEST CONTROL COMBINES ALL OF THESE THINGS.

market in 1988. Chlordane worked well in protecting structures from termite infestation, but none of the replacement chemicals were working satisfactorily. Initially discouraged, she tried other approaches to the termite problem. She began research into aboveground application using chemicals in a foam solution.

In 1995, Raytheon Services hired Hawkins to go to Johnston Atoll in the South Pacific. The island is a U.S. National Fish and Wildlife refuge, and as such, no chemicals are allowed to be placed on the ground. At that time, no one had been able to solve the termite problem on the island for more than 40 years, and she was given six months. It was the perfect laboratory to refine and test her new process.

All buildings treated by Hawkins were termite free at the end of only four months, and are still free of termites. And the chemicals she used had an extremely low toxicity, somewhere between that of aspirin and salt. Hawkins then returned to Tucson and applied what she had learned on the island to the process now used by 5 Star.

ENVIRONMENT-FRIENDLY TECHNIQUES

Called Star Foam, the process Hawkins devised works with Mother Nature and focuses on using as few chemicals as necessary to avoid pollution. The foam is more effective and less toxic than regular termite poisons, as it penetrates the food source of the termites, the wood in structures. The foam is injected into the walls through a hole the size of a small pen cap and renders the wood inedible to the termites, thus driving the colony to find food elsewhere. "It's a different approach, and it works," Hawkins says.

Today, 5 Star Termite and Pest Control is a family operation. Daughter Heidi is the human resources director, supervising payroll and employee records. She is also a full-time student at the University of Arizona, where she is pursuing a degree in public health. Daughter Gretchen is multitalented in that she can dispatch, schedule, and complete documents for state and local agencies, while handling accounting when necessary. She is also a full-time student at the university, majoring in chemical engineering. And daughter Chrissy helps with office work on weekends and is a part-time student a Pima Community College.

Hawkins predicts that her company will continue to grow in the foreseeable future. She has received inquiries from as far away as Jordan and South Africa regarding her foaming process. She also

JONATHAN POSTAL

gets frequent inquiries via the company's Web site, located at www.5star-termite.com, from all across the country. Future expansion will include additional trucks, equipment, and employees. Hawkins'

philosophy—Be honest, do good work, and take care of your customers—has caused her company to become one of the largest termite and pest control companies in the state.

BASED IN TUCSON, 5 STAR SERVES CLIENTS THROUGHOUT ARIZONA AND THE SOUTHWESTERN UNITED STATES.

JONATHAN POSTAL

WHEN GEORGIA LACY FIRST OPENED HER OWN ADVERTISING AND MARKETING AGENCY IN 1981, HER CAPITAL WAS LIMITED, BUT HER OPTIMISM WAS LIMITLESS. TODAY, GEO ADVERTISING AND MARKETING IS RECOGNIZED AS ONE

of Arizona's leading ad agencies, with clients who have ranged from southern Arizona's largest automotive dealer to the state's top privately held corporation. "Our clients respect the fact that we work hard and produce results for them," Lacy says. "As a result of our hard work, we have grown with our clients' successes."

Lacy started her career in advertising by learning media basics as a receptionist, sales secretary, and assistant to KCUB Radio owner Jim Slone. She worked at Taylor Advertising and Waller Advertising in Tucson, and later relocated to El Paso, where she worked for an agency with offices in El Paso and Ciudad Juárez.

Lacy returned to Arizona in 1981 to start her own business, opening GEO Advertising and Marketing on April 1. "It was difficult at first," she says. "The hardest part of the business was the first five years, being taken seriously." But she navigated the rough spots by focusing on quality. "Since then, pure client results have kept us together," she notes.

> "OUR CLIENTS RESPECT THE FACT THAT WE WORK HARD AND PRODUCE RESULTS FOR THEM," SAYS GEORGIA LACY, FOUNDER AND PRESIDENT OF GEO ADVERTISING AND MARKETING. "AS A RESULT OF OUR HARD WORK, WE HAVE GROWN WITH OUR CLIENTS' SUCCESSES."

INTERNATIONAL CLIENT BASE

Today, 15 GEO employees work with more than 25 clients on accounts in Arizona, New Mexico, Texas, Oklahoma, and Kentucky, as well as Mexico. The agency also maintains a satellite office in Phoenix. With her experience across the border—and the bilingual skills of GEO Vice President Theo Serrano—Lacy says her firm is able to negotiate both the U.S. and the Mexican cultures.

GEO's accounts include many of Mexico's largest developers and the tourism department of the Mexican state of Sonora. In addition, GEO devel-

(FROM LEFT) HOLLY HUMPHRIES, OFFICE MANAGER; LINDA GREGORY, MEDIA DIRECTOR; JODI WALLIN, OPERATIONS MANAGER; LACY; THEO SERRANO, VICE PRESIDENT; AND WILLIAM WORKMAN, CREATIVE DIRECTOR, MAKE UP THE CORE OF GEO.

CLOCKWISE FROM TOP LEFT:
GEO DESIGNED A FULL-COLOR,
EIGHT-PAGE BROCHURE TO ENTICE
THE INTERNATIONAL TOURISM MARKET
TO PUERTO PEÑASCO IN MEXICO.

GEO TARGETED HISPANIC HOMEBUYERS
IN TWO VERY DIFFERENT DEMOGRAPH-
ICS THROUGH TWO DIFFERENT TELEVI-
SION COMMERCIALS: ONE AIMED AT
YOUNG FAMILIES AND THE OTHER AT
RETIRED COUPLES.

GEO DESIGNED A SUPER BILLBOARD
FOR A SUPER CLIENT, SUPERCUTS.

oped a campaign for the seaside tourist destinations of Cabo San Lucas, San Carlos, and Puerto Peñasco, Mexico. The agency also works with Telemundo television in Tucson and Phoenix. Clients stick with GEO for an average of seven years—a much longer period than the industry standard. "Most of the firm's clients are generated through referrals," Lacy says.

While the firm's annual billings are more than $7 million, businesses both large and small—and with varied budgets—rely on GEO to develop their advertising. "We've had the biggest of clients to the smallest. We don't treat them any differently," Lacy says. "We're not dependent on one type of clientele."

CREATIVE SUCCESS
GEO has received several awards for its radio, print, and television campaigns, and *Arizona Business Magazine* has rated GEO one of the top 20 agencies in Arizona. "We've never really wanted to be number one," Lacy says. "We've always been in the top three in Tucson and top 20 in Arizona."

GEO is able to handle all phases of marketing, advertising, and public relations in-house. Its art department generates camera-ready art from logos to black-and-white newspaper ads to four-color brochures and ads. The firm's

creative department coordinates, writes, and produces radio and television commercials of any length, and the media department strategically places advertisements to reach target demographics. Image exposure is handled by the public relations department, which concentrates on generating media coverage of GEO's clients.

GEO prides itself on its experience in producing creative, memorable ads and targeting diverse demographics. The agency also extends one-on-one service. "When we take the time to invest in a client, we feel we become a part of their staff," Lacy says. "And if there's a last-minute project, we'll work all night, if necessary."

ANCHORED IN TUCSON
GEO benefits from its experienced staff. "Tucson has a tendency to gather creative people," Lacy says. Her staff works just as hard as it would in New York or Chicago. "Although Tucson has a slower pace, the pressure of getting an ad out is the same," she says. "But you've got the peaceful mountains and hiking in the desert. It's a great balance."

Tucson-area clients include housing developments Rancho Sahuarita and Heritage Highlands. Lacy says it's gratifying to be involved with companies that help turn vast stretches of dirt into beau-

tiful homes and golf courses, and she was especially impressed by the environmental research conducted by Heritage Highlands builder U.S. Home. The campaign developed for Heritage Highlands by GEO told prospective home owners that hiking, golfing, swimming, and tennis were right outside their front doors. Longtime clients include local radio stations The Mix, The Fan, and Mega Oldies. "There is no one out there who makes sure the customers are happier," Lacy says. "That comes through in the advertising."

In addition to her work in the advertising industry, Lacy is also active in the community, volunteering and working on several community events every year. She has also been active in the Republican Party and has served on several finance committees. Lacy is a past president of the Tucson Ad Club and a past member of the Tucson Women's Commission. She currently serves on the Boys & Girls Club board of directors and is a member of the University of Arizona Wildcat Club. Lacy was inducted into the Advertising Hall of Fame in 1986, and was named Arizona's Advertising Professional of the Year in 1991.

With its award-winning work and successful campaigns for clients, GEO is certain to continue producing results-driven advertising well into the new millennium.

W

HILE MANY PEOPLE WHO RUN SMALL, LOCAL BUSINESSES WORRY ABOUT COMPETING WITH MEGASTORES, FRED AND KATHLEEN KASPER HAVE KEPT SWS ELECTRONICS & COMPUTERS RUNNING SUCCESSFULLY FOR 17

years, sparking loyalty among customers and employees.

The company was recognized initially for servicing large OEM accounts by selling electronic components, which included a vast array of products from connectors to wire and cable. Over the years, SWS expanded its products to include manufacturing custom cable assemblies, and later offered retail products for consumer electronics/components and computers. In addition, SWS now offers value-added computers, network stations, multimedia systems, and the largest local selection of computer products and peripherals, as well as computer repair service and upgrades on- or off-site. "Networking is a particular strength," says Fred H. Kasper Sr., president of SWS. "We're better at networking than anyone in town because we perform the total job."

SWS is an alternative to other computer stores—large or small—because the service-oriented staff is trained to create solutions for the customer. According to

the Kaspers, the company is run with a Tucson mentality, not a huge corporate mentality.

A FOUNDATION FOR QUALITY

Established in 1982 as Southwest Sales, the business eventually was incorporated in 1988 and took the name SWS Electronics, eventually adding Computers to the company's name and expertise. At first, the company mainly served the University of Arizona and other businesses by selling electronic components and manufacturing specialized custom cable assemblies. A big part of the company's business is cable assembly because SWS is one of only a few companies with the flexibility to make cables in odd sizes. Today, SWS is dedicated to many different areas of electronic sales and service.

The Kaspers first came to Tucson to attend the University of Arizona. Charmed by the weather, the sense of small-town friendliness, and the prospect of year-round golf, they decided to stay. "We fell in love with the Tucson community and decided we would never leave," says Vice President Kathleen Kasper.

In 1992, SWS bought land on Plumer Avenue and eventually built a 12,000-square-foot facility, which now houses the retail store as well as a large computer repair center and custom cable assembly space. The new facility allowed the company to begin retailing computers and thousands of parts and product lines. "The minute we went retail, we

started getting calls for computers," says Kathleen Kasper. "Ever since the expansion, we have been satisfying the needs and demands of our customers."

SWS also aims to treat its customers like good friends. One of the ways the company accommodates its customers' needs is by completing repairs faster than many other businesses. The company's strengths also include its return policy, ability to offer quality parts and services for reasonable prices, and knowledgeable staff. "We can and will help our customers find what they need to solve their problem," says an SWS computer technician.

In the future, SWS Electronics & Computers plans to expand by attracting small businesses and offering them on-site service. In addition, SWS has an E-commerce Web site—www.sws-electronics.com—that offers reliable services to on-line customers, from novices to professionals. SWS also offers a reseller/corporate plan for competitive pricing for the knowledgeable professional buyer or reseller of computer parts and systems.

"There's nobody that can give them the kind of service SWS can give them," says Kathleen Kasper. Once customers get hooked on the extensive selection of parts to complete the total job, whether it's electronic, computer, cable, or networking related, the Kaspers are sure customers realize the truth of the company's slogan: "SWS . . . there is no substitute."

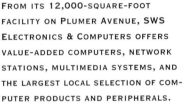

FROM ITS 12,000-SQUARE-FOOT FACILITY ON PLUMER AVENUE, SWS ELECTRONICS & COMPUTERS OFFERS VALUE-ADDED COMPUTERS, NETWORK STATIONS, MULTIMEDIA SYSTEMS, AND THE LARGEST LOCAL SELECTION OF COMPUTER PRODUCTS AND PERIPHERALS.

▲ PHILIP RAMACKERS

▲ PHILIP RAMACKERS

**A**GAINST THE DRAMATIC BACKDROP OF THE SANTA CATALINA FOOTHILLS, ANCIENT SAGUAROS LIFT THEIR ARMS TO THE SKY. COTTONTAIL RABBITS AND COVEYS OF QUAIL SCURRY IN THE UNDERBRUSH. COYOTES CALL TO EACH

other, their voices echoing across the high Sonoran Desert. Nestled within this pristine setting is The Lodge at Ventana Canyon, ranked by *Condé Nast Traveler* as the Southwest's best golf resort. At this lushly secluded hideaway, 50 spacious guest suites are surrounded by 600 acres of extraordinary natural beauty in open space that provides a habitat for deer, red-tailed hawks, and other desert natives.

Meandering through the mystical canyons and arroyos are Tom Fazio's two 18-hole championship Ventana Canyon courses, which have won *Golf Magazine*'s Silver Medal Award and *Links Magazine*'s Best of Golf Award. The Mountain course features the celebrated third hole—the most photographed hole west of the Mississippi—which offers a breathtaking panorama that stretches 100 miles south into Mexico. The Canyon course winds through the inspiring beauty of Esperero Canyon and incorporates the massive Whaleback Rock, where at night, bobcats emerge from the desert to wander among the greens.

Other recreational pleasures include a fitness center open around the clock, 12 lighted tennis courts, men's and women's saunas and whirlpool spas, and a sports swimming center. Nature walks and trail hikes reveal the wonders of Ventana Canyon, known as a spiritual haven to long-ago desert dwellers, who left their petroglyphs on nearby walls of stone. And hot-air balloon rides, desert jeep tours, and horseback rides let guests enjoy

panoramic views of the majestic desert surrounding the resort.

The Lodge reflects the spirit of warmth and comfort cherished by western travelers. Amid the natural pageantry of Ventana Canyon, the relaxing intimacy is enhanced by contemporary mission-inspired furniture softened with Anasazi-design cushions, a collection of southwestern treasures, and the massive fieldstone fireplace soaring toward the lobby's atrium skylight.

Guest suites capitalize on the spectacular views with spacious terraces, and offer 800 to 1,500 square feet of homelike comfort, including a lavishly stocked, in-room refreshment center and one or two bedrooms with king-size beds. Among the memorable touches are a spiral stair-

case to the two-bedroom loft, and large baths with telephones, plush terry cloth robes, and often an old-fashioned footed bathtub.

Both the Hearthstone dining room and the Sierra Bar offer panoramic vistas of the Catalina foothills, the golf course, and the lush, green mesquite trees, palo verdes, and saguaros that line the shadowed chasms of Ventana Canyon. Just outside, the Sabino Terrace dining area is frequented by quail, chuckwallas, and other desert dwellers that make themselves at home around the resort.

It's just the kind of harmony with nature that guests have come to expect from the Wyndham Luxury Resorts, and it's surrounded by a uniquely magical setting at The Lodge at Ventana Canyon.

RECREATIONAL PLEASURES AT THE LODGE AT VENTANA CANYON INCLUDE NATURE WALKS AND TRAIL HIKES THAT REVEAL THE WONDERS OF THE CANYON, KNOWN AS A SPIRITUAL HAVEN TO LONG-AGO DESERT DWELLERS, WHO LEFT THEIR PETROGLYPHS ON NEARBY WALLS OF STONE. AND HOT-AIR BALLOON RIDES, DESERT JEEP TOURS, AND HORSEBACK RIDES LET GUESTS ENJOY PANORAMIC VIEWS OF THE MAJESTIC DESERT SURROUNDING THE RESORT (TOP).

NESTLED WITHIN THE PRISTINE SETTING OF THE SANTA CATALINA FOOTHILLS IS THE LODGE AT VENTANA CANYON, WHERE 50 SPACIOUS GUEST SUITES ARE SURROUNDED BY 600 ACRES OF EXTRAORDINARY NATURAL BEAUTY IN OPEN SPACE THAT PROVIDES A HABITAT FOR DEER, RED-TAILED HAWKS, AND OTHER DESERT NATIVES (BOTTOM LEFT AND RIGHT).

I N RESPONSE TO A GROWING COMMUNITY'S NEED FOR CONVENIENT, QUALITY HEALTH CARE, NORTHWEST MEDICAL CENTER (NMC) OPENED ITS DOORS IN 1983 TO AWAITING NEIGHBORS ON TUCSON'S NORTH-WEST SIDE. BY OFFERING A FULL SPECTRUM OF HEALTH CARE

services, NMC has played a leading role in the tremendous growth of the northwest community. Tucson's northwest side now reports the largest continued growth in Pima County—new families, schools, and businesses—and NMC is growing with it.

A RECOGNIZED LEADER IN HEALTH CARE

Northwest Medical Center is a 193-bed, full-service health care facility with 1,100 employees and more than 600 physicians on staff. With a community population ranging from young families to retirees, NMC offers its patients comprehensive care in obstetrics, orthopedics, pulmonology, gynecology, neurology, cardiology, cardiopulmonology, oncology, ophthalmology, and gerontology.

Especially unique to Northwest Medical Center is its Pediatric Urgent Care. This center was created to fulfill the need of working parents whose schedules may not always coincide with

their child's pediatrician. The Pediatric Urgent Care is open evenings and weekends, and is staffed with a board-certified pediatrician.

Fulfilling its mission to become a leader in progressive health care, NMC boasts the regionally recognized HeartCare Center, the Center for Neuroscience, and the Women's Health Center.

The Regional HeartCare Center at Northwest Medical Center offers highly skilled heart specialist teams and the most advanced diagnostic tools and techniques available for preventive, rehabilitative, and emergency care. Northwest Medical Center was the first hospital in Tucson to perform endoscopic vein retrieval for coronary bypass patients. This less invasive procedure allows patients to heal more quickly and with less pain.

While prevention is still the best medicine and surgery is always the last resort, NMC is a community leader in utilizing technology and less invasive procedures when treating surgical patients.

For example, the Center for Neuroscience has developed the BrainLab, a computerized, three-dimensional, image-guided surgery with cordless instruments for brain surgery patients. In addition, the Center for Neuroscience is one of the few hospitals nationwide to use micro-endoscopic discectomy (MED), a surgical procedure that has revolutionized back surgery.

The first freestanding medical center in southern Arizona devoted exclusively to women's health, the Women's Health Center deals with the health issues of women of all ages. Patients receive both inpatient and outpatient services, including obstetrics, gynecology, and mammography, as well as complete state-of-the-art diagnostic services.

Residents of Tucson's northwest side are offered a full range of services and programs all conveniently located on the NMC campus. Patients and their families are assured quality care in all these areas: emergency services, adult

FOUNDED IN 1983, NORTHWEST MEDICAL CENTER (NMC) IS A 193-BED, FULL-SERVICE HEALTH CARE FACILITY WITH 1,100 EMPLOYEES AND MORE THAN 600 PHYSICIANS ON STAFF.

and pediatric urgent care, intensive care, surgical services, ambulatory services, and MRI/CT scan/nuclear medicine.

HEALTH CARE PROFESSIONALS CHOOSE NMC

Northwest Medical Center has become the hospital of choice for many physicians and health care practitioners in Tucson. It is the commitment to state-of-the-art technology, continuing staff education, and quality care that attracts physicians and specialists to practice at NMC. The supportive, caring environment nurtures the professional relationship between physician and staff, which enhances patient care and promotes positive medical outcomes.

CARING FOR THE COMMUNITY

Northwest Medical Center has become a health care leader in the Tucson area because of its strong ties to the community. Many of the programs developed at NMC are the result of a continuous dia-

logue between the medical center and its many community advisory boards.

Northwest Medical Center, in partnership with Marana, Amphitheater, and Flowing Wells school districts, offers free health care to children in need. The program, Care for Kids, provides emergency and urgent care as well as back-to-school immunizations and athletic physicals to children referred to NMC by school health professionals.

As part of the surrounding areas' school curricula, NMC created a field-trip program for area fifth-graders. Students tour the hospital and speak with employees from all departments to learn that there is more to hospital work than just medicine.

Community health education is a priority for NMC, and the staff seeks opportunities to share information with its neighbors. Community health education programs are offered on important and timely health topics at a variety of locations, and the NMC Physician Referral Call Center provides an invaluable

service to both newcomers and native Tucsonans. The center helps connect patients with physicians according to their personal and medical needs.

For individuals 55 and older, NMC offers Senior Friends. This program promotes good health through education, prevention training, health screenings, and recreational activities. In addition, NMC offers volunteer opportunities throughout the facility for seniors and young adults.

Northwest Medical Center is accredited by the Joint Commission on Accreditation of Healthcare Organizations (JCAHO), and has been serving the medical needs of Tucson for almost 20 years. Although much has changed in health care and the community of northwest Tucson, NMC's commitment remains focused on providing quality, cost-effective health care.

The services of Northwest Medical Center will continue to be a reflection of the growth and needs of the community it serves.

WITH ITS COMMITMENT TO STATE-OF-THE-ART TECHNOLOGY, CONTINUING STAFF EDUCATION, AND QUALITY CARE, NORTHWEST MEDICAL CENTER HAS BECOME THE HOSPITAL OF CHOICE FOR HEALTH CARE PRACTITIONERS IN TUCSON (TOP LEFT).

NORTHWEST MEDICAL CENTER IS A COMMUNITY LEADER IN UTILIZING TECHNOLOGY AND LESS INVASIVE PROCEDURES WHEN TREATING SURGICAL PATIENTS (TOP RIGHT).

THE SUPPORTIVE, CARING ENVIRONMENT AT NORTHWEST MEDICAL CENTER NURTURES THE PROFESSIONAL RELATIONSHIP BETWEEN PHYSICIAN AND STAFF, WHICH ENHANCES PATIENT CARE AND PROMOTES POSITIVE MEDICAL OUTCOMES (BOTTOM LEFT AND RIGHT).

HENEVER A BUSINESS DISCOVERS THAT THERE MAY BE A LEAK IN ITS TANKS OR PIPING, CHANCES ARE THAT TRACER RESEARCH CORPORATION CAN FIND AND FIX IT. "WE USE TECHNOLOGY TO TEST UNDERGROUND TANKS

and piping, as well as aboveground tanks," says Shannon Marty, Tracer's chief executive officer.

Since 1983, Tracer Research has provided environmental services to owners and operators of underground and aboveground tanks and piping at more than 10,000 refineries, pipeline terminals, tank farms, military bases, airports, gas stations, and chemical manufacturing plants throughout North America, Europe, the Caribbean, and the Pacific Rim.

ROOTED IN RESEARCH

Tracer Research began as a small environmental company that pioneered the commercial application of soil gas surveys. The company was founded by a University of Arizona hydrology professor, Dr. Glenn Thompson, who analyzed an industrial site where the chemical trichloroethylene (TCE) had seeped into groundwater. Dr. Thompson pioneered a method to detect the plume of contamination that was both less expensive and

easier to apply than traditional investigative methods.

Initially, Tracer focused on environmental sampling, but today, the company does more leak detection. "We're expanding our capabilities," Marty says. "There are a lot of technologies that we've invented and developed, and there are others that we've brought into our toolbox that add value to commercial operations."

The company's work includes projects that help preserve aboveground storage tanks that are corroding on the bottom. "Our solution is a lot less expensive, and can substantially extend the lives of the tanks," says Marty.

TRACER TECHNOLOGY

Tracer Research developed the patented Tracer Tight® leak detection method for underground and aboveground storage tanks and pipelines. The Tracer Tight leak detection test is one of the industry's most sensitive and reliable tests for leaks in underground and aboveground tanks and piping. "We have the only technology

that allows you to test your system while it's still in service," Marty says. "We do a lot of work with the military and commercial airports because we provide a system that will perform without interrupting site operations."

In addition to the Tucson headquarters, Tracer has offices in California, Colorado, Georgia, Missouri, New Jersey, and Texas, as well as an international presence in London. With a staff of 100, Tracer hires engineers, geologists, hydrologists, chemists, industrial hygienists, laboratory analysts, field technicians, technical writers, and mathematicians. Tracer employees have undergone Occupational Safety and Health Administration (OSHA) health and safety training, and have received specific training required by the company's client base.

"Tracer's corporate headquarters is in beautiful Tucson, quite a distance from the majority of tanks and pipeline systems," says Marty. "However, the benefits of living here are great for our employees."

HEADQUARTERED IN TUCSON, TRACER RESEARCH CORPORATION PROVIDES ENVIRONMENTAL SERVICES TO OWNERS AND OPERATORS OF UNDERGROUND AND ABOVEGROUND TANKS AND PIPING AT MORE THAN 10,000 REFINERIES, PIPELINE TERMINALS, TANK FARMS, MILITARY BASES, AIRPORTS, GAS STATIONS, AND CHEMICAL MANUFACTURING PLANTS THROUGHOUT NORTH AMERICA, EUROPE, THE CARIBBEAN, AND THE PACIFIC RIM.

U S WEST HAS A LONG HISTORY IN ARIZONA, DATING BACK MORE THAN 100 YEARS TO THE VERY FIRST TELEPHONE SERVICE IN THE TERRITORY. TODAY, U S WEST CONSIDERS ITSELF MORE THAN THE LOCAL PHONE COMPANY. FROM

telephony to the Internet and on-line services, U S WEST aims to make life better for millions of customers in Arizona through integrated solutions, new and innovative products, and superior service. "U S WEST is all about simplifying the way people communicate, now and in the future," says Bill Stack, general manager of U S WEST-Arizona.

With more than 190,000 miles of fiber-optic cable and 2.6 million telephone lines connecting telephone customers throughout Arizona, U S WEST is wired for the future. Each day, U S WEST adds nearly 600 telephone lines and invests $1 million in new equipment and facilities, from high-speed digital networks that provide quick access to the Internet to self-healing networks that ensure reliable service.

INVESTING IN ARIZONA

In all, U S WEST has invested more than $4 billion in equipment and property in Arizona. Part of this investment has gone to building top-notch facilities, including more than 200 central offices that ensure reliable service throughout the state. Perhaps U S WEST's greatest investment

is its workforce of more than 6,400 employees, who provide integrated communications solutions to about 1.6 million businesses and residential customers.

As the largest telecommunications company in the state, U S WEST has the unique capacity to provide one-stop shopping by bundling a broad range of products and services, including local, long-distance, wireless, and data. U S WEST also was the first to deploy the next generation of wireless telephone service. Advanced PCS (personal communication service) offers one-number integration, allowing customers to use the same number as their home or office phone. As high-speed data services move into the 21st century, U S WEST is working to make Web tone as readily available as dial tone. U S WEST MegaBit Services offers high-speed data connections up to 250 times faster than the typical dial-up modem, all over existing phone lines.

FUTURE OF TELECOMMUNICATIONS

In addition to advanced products and services, U S WEST customers benefit from upgrades in the telecommunications network. One such enhancement is Network 21, a $32 million, self-healing network that instantaneously identifies phone line disruptions and reroutes phone calls and data transmissions.

As a business leader, U S WEST takes its role in the community seriously. Each year, the company contributes more than $3 million to support education, arts and culture, economic development, and health and human services in Arizona. Beyond corporate giving, the Arizona workforce of U S WEST volunteers more than 9,000 hours each year at more than 50 charitable organizations.

Through research and development and strategic marketing alliances, U S WEST is positioned to stay in the forefront of technological advances. In the years to come, U S WEST will continue to focus on the needs of its customers and provide them with telecommunications solutions to make their lives better.

U S WEST CHOICE TV & ONLINE IS THE FIRST TECHNOLOGY OF ITS KIND TO INTEGRATE DIGITAL TELEVISION, TELEPHONY, AND HIGH-SPEED INTERNET ACCESS USING EXISTING TELEPHONE LINES (TOP RIGHT).

FROM TELEPHONY AND THE INTERNET TO DIGITAL TELEVISION AND ON-LINE SERVICES, U S WEST IS WORKING TO MAKE LIFE BETTER FOR MILLIONS OF CUSTOMERS IN ARIZONA THROUGH INTEGRATED SOLUTIONS, NEW AND INNOVATIVE PRODUCTS, AND SUPERIOR SERVICE (BOTTOM RIGHT).

WITH MORE THAN 190,000 MILES OF FIBER-OPTIC CABLE AND 2.6 MILLION TELEPHONE LINES CONNECTING CUSTOMERS THROUGHOUT ARIZONA, U S WEST IS WIRED FOR THE FUTURE.

T

HE NAME IS DIFFERENT, BUT THE BUSINESS IS THE SAME. HONEYWELL INTERNATIONAL INC.—FORMERLY KNOWN AS ALLIEDSIGNAL INC.—HAS ENJOYED A LONG AND SUCCESSFUL HISTORY IN TUCSON. THE TWO COMPANIES MERGED IN DECEMBER

1999, and AlliedSignal adopted the well-known Honeywell name.

This advanced technology and manufacturing company serves customers worldwide with aerospace and automotive products, chemicals, fibers, plastics, and high-tech materials, among other things. At the company's Oro Valley facility, located on 30 acres at the base of the Santa Catalina Mountains, about 850 employees design, manufacture, and test mainly electronic products for commercial, general aviation, and military markets.

While the public doesn't see most of Honeywell's products, it counts on the company to support such diverse fields as aerospace, pharmaceutical, fiber optics, and home environmental controls. The Tucson facility's products include engine controllers, air data controls, sensors, cabin pressure systems, smoke detectors, and electric power generators. The site

MOVING INTO THE 21ST CENTURY, HONEYWELL INTERNATIONAL INC.'S TUCSON FACILITY CONTINUES TO STRIVE FOR EXCELLENCE, BUILDING ON ITS LONG HISTORY OF GROWTH AND SUCCESS TO BECOME ONE OF THE PREMIER COMPANIES IN THE WORLD.

does mainly commercial work, with about 21 percent military and 4 percent space work. Customers include Boeing/McDonnell Douglas, the U.S. military, General Electric, and Lockheed Martin.

Honeywell in Tucson takes great pride in its safety record, and in 1998, reached a record 9.5 million hours without a lost workday case—the best in the company. Tucson employees also take care of their community, with many volunteering for several organizations and schools. The company has also been recognized for its contributions to United Way.

AN ILLUSTRIOUS HISTORY

The company traces its history back more than 75 years. During World War I, Germany controlled much of the world's chemical industry, causing shortages of commodities like dyes and drugs. That prompted *Washington Post* publisher Eugene Meyer and scientist William Nichols to form Allied Chemical & Dye Corporation in 1920, an amalgamation of five American chemical companies that had been established in the 1800s.

The company's first venture into new markets came in 1928, when it opened a synthetic ammonia plant near Hopewell, and became the world's leading producer of ammonia. After World War II, the company began manufacturing other new products, including nylon 6—used in everything from tires to clothes—and refrigerants. In 1958, the company changed its name to Allied Chemical Corporation and moved into its current corporate headquarters in Morristown, New Jersey.

In 1962, Allied bought Union Texas Natural Gas, which owned oil and gas properties throughout the Americas. At first, Allied considered it mainly a supplier of raw materials for its chemical products. However, that changed in the early 1970s, when CEO John Connor (who had been secretary of commerce under President Lyndon Johnson) sold many of the company's unprofitable businesses and invested in oil and gas exploration. By the time Edward Hennessy Jr. became CEO in 1979, Union Texas was responsible for 80 percent of Allied's income.

After changing its name to Allied Corporation in 1981, the company bought the Bendix Corporation, an aerospace and automotive company, in 1983. By 1984, Bendix was generating half of Allied's income, while oil and gas was generating 38 percent.

In 1985, Allied merged with the Signal Companies, adding to its aerospace, automotive, and engineered materials businesses. Founded by Sam Mosher in 1922 as the Signal Gasoline Company, Signal was originally a California company that produced gasoline from natural gas. In 1928, the company changed its name to Signal Oil & Gas and began oil production. Signal then merged with the Garrett Corporation, a Los Angeles-based aerospace company, and in 1968, adopted the Signal Companies as its corporate name.

The addition of Signal's Garrett division to Bendix made aerospace the largest business sector for Allied-Signal. The company sold 50 percent of Union Texas in 1985, and a year later, it divested 35 non-

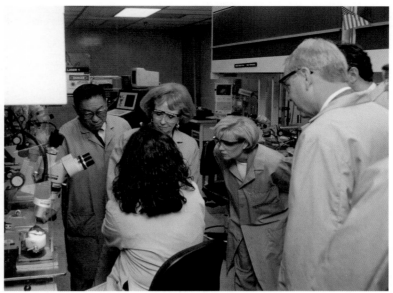

strategic businesses through the formation and spin-off of the Henley Group, Inc.

MOVING TOWARD THE FUTURE

Allied-Signal began a comprehensive overhaul in mid-1991 under the leadership of its new CEO, Larry Bossidy. The company improved cash flow and operating margins, increased productivity, and sought to form the company into a global competitive force. In 1992, the company bought Westinghouse Electric's copper laminates business and sold its remaining interest in Union Texas. In 1993, the company's name was changed to AlliedSignal to reinforce a one-company image and to signify the full integration of all of its businesses.

Today, as Honeywell, the company employs more than 70,000 people in 40 countries, and had $14.5 billion in sales in 1998. It ranks among the top 100 of the Fortune 500 and is one of the 30 companies that makes up the Dow Jones Industrial Average.

Recently, Honeywell was named the number one diversified company by *Forbes Global* magazine and one of the best places to work by *Fortune* magazine, an honor the company has won before. Bossidy was named CEO of the year by *Chief Executive* magazine in 1998. Under Bossidy's leadership, the company has achieved a total return on stock of 508 percent, increased productivity at an average annual rate of nearly 6 percent, and experienced 26 consecutive quarters of earning increases of 14 percent or more.

Moving into the 21st century, Allied-Signal celebrated its merger with Honeywell and the partnership of two great leaders—Bossidy and Honeywell CEO Mike Bonsignore, who has assumed leadership of the company as CEO. Honeywell International is an organization that will continue to strive for excellence, building on a long history of growth and success to become one of the premier companies in the world.

IN MAY 1999, ARIZONA GOVERNOR JANE DEE HULL TOURED THE HONEYWELL FACILITIES—THEN ALLIEDSIGNAL INC.—AND WAS TREATED TO A LESSON ON THE COMPANY'S WORK IN CABIN PRESSURE AND SENSORS.

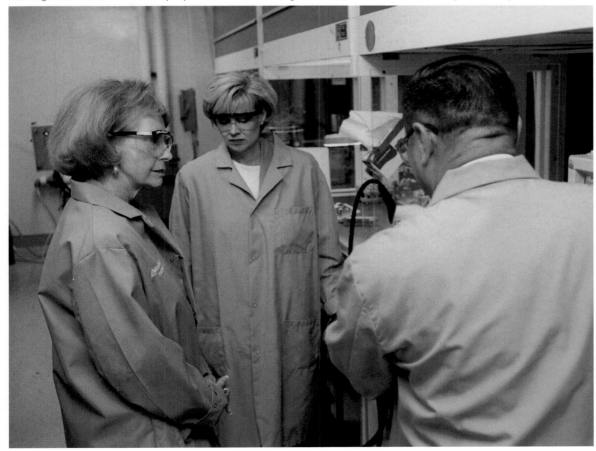

ANCER IS THE SECOND-LEADING CAUSE OF DEATH IN THE UNITED STATES, CLAIMING 550,000 LIVES EVERY YEAR. ABOUT 10 MILLION PEOPLE IN THE UNITED STATES HAVE A HISTORY OF INVASIVE CANCER, AND 1.4 MILLION NEW CASES OF INVASIVE

cancer are diagnosed each year.

Ventana Medical Systems, Inc. is on the front line of the battle against cancer, developing instruments and reagent systems that help determine diagnosis and treatment. "The earlier the condition is diagnosed, the greater the chances of a successful therapeutic outcome," says Pierre Sice, vice president and chief financial officer.

IMPROVING TEST RESULTS

Ventana's products automate the preparation and staining of cells and tissues, which reduce the amount of human error introduced into these tests. Says Sice, "Everything we do has to do with tissue." The company's objective is to automate all of the work cells in the hospital histology lab. In that pursuit, it manufactures tissue processors to prepare and preserve tissue, microtomes to cut tissue, and instruments and reagent systems to perform immunohistochemistry, special stain, and in situ hybridization tests on tissue. Immunohistochemistry is used for the diagnosis of cancer, while special stains also are used to detect bacterial, viral, or connective tissue disorder conditions.

Until recently, these tests were performed by individuals, but the complexity of the process has led to inconsistent results. Performed manually, immuno-histochemistry requires skilled technical

personnel to perform as many as 60 individual steps and can take several days to complete. Each step must be performed in the proper sequence and for the right length of time. Ventana's automated systems improve reliability, reproducibility, and consistency of test results. Turnaround time is also faster, and since there is less need for skilled lab technicians, it keeps labor costs down.

"The manual process is time consuming," Sice says. "But by automating, you can achieve quality, consistency, and labor savings." For example, testing sometimes requires the application of heat, which can fluctuate several degrees when applied by hand. By machine, heat applications are much more precise.

People have not been completely removed from the equation, however. "Interpretation and diagnosis are still the domain of the pathologist," says Sice. "These systems have optimized the interaction between instrument and reagent. They are optimized for the pathologist's review. If the slides are more consistently stained, you're going to get a more consistent diagnosis."

The faster and more accurate the diagnosis, the better the survival rate of the patient. Health care professionals are increasing their use of screening and early detection programs because it's less expensive and more effective to treat cancer when it's caught early. Thanks in part to early detection and treatment,

the mortality rates of certain cancers have dropped.

FIGHTING THE BATTLE AGAINST CANCER

In 1985, Dr. Thomas Grogan, a professor of pathology at the University of Arizona Medical Center, sought to overcome the inconsistent quality of the slides he was asked to read as a pathologist. In order to try to eliminate those inconsistencies, he founded Ventana Medical Systems, Inc. Today, Grogan still sits on the company's board of directors.

In 1991, Ventana began selling its first system, the Ventana 320 instrument, and related reagents used for automated immunohistochemistry tests. Since then, Ventana has introduced the Ventana ES—the successor to the 320—and the Ventana Gen II. In August 1997, Ventana introduced the NexES IHC as a successor to the ES, followed by the NexES SS in October 1998, which has been well received for its modular design and operating efficiency.

Ventana's products are in use at the University of Arizona Medical Center and at 38 of the 42 top cancer research centers in the United States, including the Mayo Clinic, Dana-Farber Cancer Institute, Johns Hopkins University, M.D. Anderson Cancer Center, Fred Hutchinson Cancer Center, and Memorial Sloan-Kettering Cancer Center. With offices in Europe and Japan, Ventana

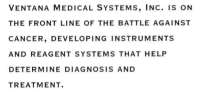

VENTANA MEDICAL SYSTEMS, INC. IS ON THE FRONT LINE OF THE BATTLE AGAINST CANCER, DEVELOPING INSTRUMENTS AND REAGENT SYSTEMS THAT HELP DETERMINE DIAGNOSIS AND TREATMENT.

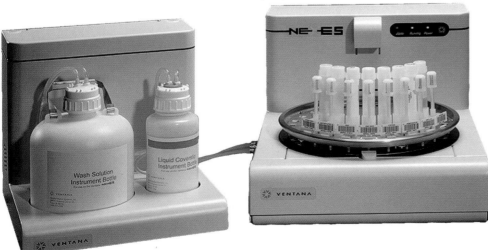

also serves overseas markets. The company believes there's a worldwide market for 6,000 of Ventana's automated immunohistochemistry instruments and 8,000 of Ventana's special stains instruments.

"We're the only company that offers true walk-away automation," Sice says. "Most of the other products on the market require a larger quantity of steps to be performed before the automation process takes over."

In the future, Ventana aims to create a product that can permit the identification of a tumor's genes to determine whether they are cancerous. The company also plans to continue to convert the immunohistochemistry market from manual to automated testing, automate other slide-staining activities, and exploit Ventana's slide-staining technology in other diagnostic labs.

In addition, the company wants to promote the use of immunohistochemistry testing instead of cultures for infectious diseases. Ventana's testing system can do in hours what takes days with culture.

The faster the disease diagnosis, the faster the patient can be treated and the lower the cost of isolating the patient.

"Ventana has developed a strong cadre of engineers and scientists," says Sice. "We've brought quite a number of individuals from other parts of the country." For Ventana and its 400 employees, Tucson is a good place to launch their battle against cancer.

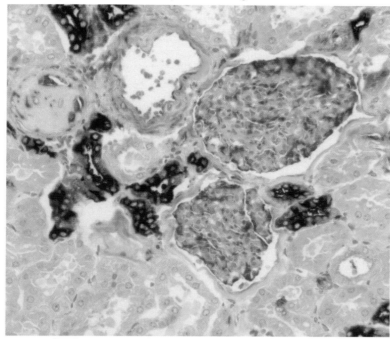

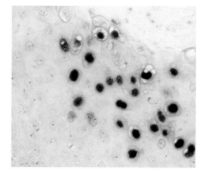

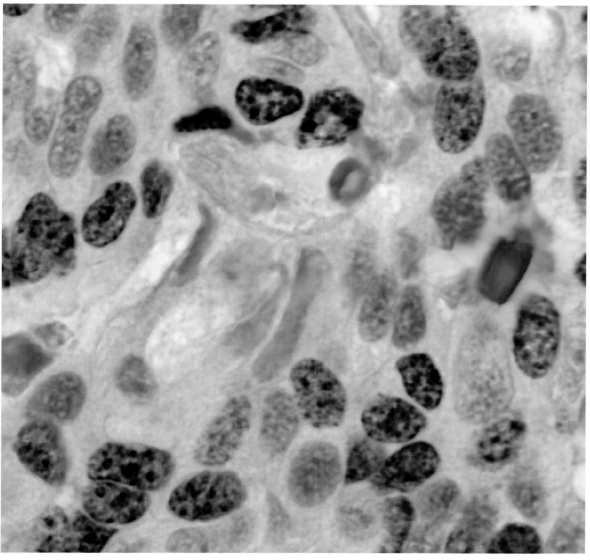

CLOCKWISE FROM TOP:
KIDNEY TISSUE STAINED WITH IHC IMMUNOHISTOCHEMISTRY MARKS SHOWING ANTI-VIMENTIN STAINING RED AND ANTI-EMA (EPITHELIAL MEMBRANE ANTIGEN) STAINING BROWN (COUNTERSTAINED WITH METHYLENE BLUE)

CERVICAL TISSUE STAINED FOR HPV (HUMAN PAPILLOMAVIRUS) USING IN SITU HYBRIDIZATION

BREAST TUMOR STAINED WITH TWO PROGNOSTIC MARKERS, SHOWING ESTROGEN RECEPTOR POSITIVE CELLS STAINING BROWN AND KI-67 POSITIVE CELLS STAINING RED

THE SONORAN DESERT PROVIDES A UNIQUE SETTING FOR THE DISTINCTIVE CONTEMPORARY DESIGNS OF GROMATZKY DUPREE AND ASSOCIATES SOUTHWEST LLC (GDA). THE ARCHITECTURE AND PLANNING FIRM, WITH OFFICES IN DALLAS AND PHOENIX,

established the Tucson office in 1986, and has enjoyed steady growth in its client base and diversity of project types and services. Architecture for business is the focus of GDA. To each project, the firm brings broad experience in the design of business facilities for performance and function, and the ability to select building materials and details that address the intense climate of the desert. This results in a forward-looking architecture that responds to the region and reflects the character and mission of the business.

COMMITMENT, EXCELLENCE, AND RESULTS

Kevin Morrow, principal, believes that GDA's philosophy has propelled the Tucson office to the forefront of commercial architecture in southern Arizona. Supported by a parent company that employs a professional staff of more than 50 people and holds licenses in 48 states, the Tucson office of GDA benefits from the diversity of services provided by a large organization, while maintaining the ability to offer each client the individual attention and service associated with a smaller firm.

Central to GDA's focus on architecture for business are the firm's efforts to assist members of the business community in meeting their facility requirements from the initial stages of site selection and evaluation through the planning and design phases to completion of the building project. Site evaluation includes an analysis of the constraints posed by

the requirements of local jurisdictions, including environmental and contextual factors, the economic viability of developing the site and building, and the potential for marketing and future use of the project. GDA's ongoing relationship with the real estate community fosters a

clear understanding of current building trends and facility requirements.

As a forerunner in the design-build process, GDA has refined the team approach to the building project. Once a building site is under consideration, GDA produces programming and schematic

ONE OF GROMATZKY DUPREE AND ASSOCIATES' (GDA) RECENT PROJECTS OF NOTE IS THE AMERICA ONLINE (AOL) OFFICE BUILDING, WHICH WON THE 1999 CONCRETE BUILDING OF THE YEAR AWARD FROM THE ARIZONA CONTRACTORS ASSOCIATION.

NATIONAL EXPOSURE AND REPUTATION HAVE PROVIDED GDA WITH THE OPPORTUNITY TO DESIGN CORPORATE FACILITIES FOR SUCH ORGANIZATIONS AS INTUIT (BOTTOM LEFT) AND MCCULLOCH (BOTTOM RIGHT).

designs that are reviewed by the owner and selected contractors. Building system alternatives, which respond to the owner's program as developer or user, are evaluated in view of budget, performance, and availability. This process ensures that the owner realizes a value-added project.

National exposure and a solid reputation for design solutions have provided GDA with the opportunity to design facilities for such organizations as Intuit, America Online, McCulloch, Qantas, United Airlines, UPS, Parker Hannifin, Kaman Aerospace, Raytheon, Nestlé Co., and John Hancock, as well as Tucson-based companies including R&R Products, Manufacturing & Research, Inc., and Southwest Door Co. GDA's design portfolio has grown steadily over the years, and includes office, manufacturing, and distribution facilities, as well as medical, health care, and retail architecture. The Tucson office has experienced regional expansion, including projects located in New Mexico and California.

One of GDA's recent projects of note is the America Online (AOL) office building in Tucson, which won the 1999 Concrete Building of the Year award from

the Arizona Contractor's Association. The design was influenced by AOL's strong corporate image of a technologically progressive company. The building has large, open office areas with views available to all employees. The structure incorporates contemporary materials, including concrete tilt panel walls, steel structures, and expansive areas of glass. Design responses to the climate are achieved by the integration of steel sun shading, site-cast concrete wing walls supporting steel trellises, and high-performance glass. AOL's response

following occupancy of the facility was to immediately commission GDA to design a new building for a second Tucson location.

GDA is looking forward to continued success in building partnerships within the business community. With a proven track record of planning and design, GDA is committed to meeting the needs of its clients by providing state-of-the-art architecture fitting into the unique landscape of the southwest.

THE AUSTERE MAJESTY OF THE DESERT PROVIDES THE PERFECT SETTING FOR THE WESTIN LA PALOMA, A 250-ACRE RESORT NESTLED AT THE BASE OF THE SANTA CATALINA MOUNTAINS. THE 487-ROOM LUXURY RESORT COMBINES SPACIOUS CONFERENCE and banquet facilities with a 27-hole, Jack Nicklaus Signature golf course; tennis and racquetball courts; swimming pools; a 177-foot water slide; three spas; a swim-up bar; and a complete health club.

"The Westin La Paloma is regarded as one of Tucson's gems," says Nancy Allison, director of marketing communications. "Local residents bring their guests, families, and friends visiting from out of town. It's considered one of the loveliest spots in Tucson."

The resort is owned by Caesar Park Hotels & Resorts, Inc., a subsidiary of Aoki Corporation, and managed by Westin Hotels and Resorts. La Paloma currently employs a dedicated staff of more than 600 under the direction of General Manager Steve Shalit.

"Opened in 1986, La Paloma was built by developers and brothers George and David Mehl. Until then, Tucson was mainly known for its guest ranches, and the brothers felt the time was right for the city to take a bigger slice of the tourism pie," Allison says. "In addition to the year-round activities offered in Tucson and southern Arizona, the Westin name helps to draw people to the resort when travelers go to make vacation plans."

A FIRST-CLASS DESTINATION

The Westin La Paloma has been recognized for its excellence by publications ranging from *Condé Nast Traveler* to *Successful Meetings*. "Travelers worldwide consider La Paloma to be one of the finest resorts within the travel industry," Allison says. In fact, the Readers' Choice Awards compiled by *Condé Nast Traveler* have ranked the hotel as one of the world's top 100 elite names in travel, one of the top 20 best resorts in the continental United States, and one of the country's top 50 golf resorts.

In 1987, after being open for less than a year, the resort received a four-star rating from the *Mobil Travel Guide*, followed by a four-diamond designation from the *American Automobile Association TourBook*. La Paloma has received these prestigious ratings every year to date. *Successful Meetings* magazine has also given La Paloma its Pinnacle Award, based on the votes of meeting planners nationwide. Further recognition has come from *Meetings and Conventions, Corporate and Incentive Travel*, and *Corporate Meetings & Incentives* magazines.

According to *Golf Digest*, the Jack Nicklaus golf course at La Paloma is one of the top 75 resort courses in the country and one of the top 10 courses in Arizona. In addition, *Golf, Golf for Women, Golfweek*, and *Golf Resort Guide* all recognize the course as one of the best in the country, and *Golf Shop Operations* has even ranked the La Paloma Golf Shop as one of the top 100 in the country.

ATMOSPHERE AND ATTITUDE

From the start, La Paloma's designers endeavored to preserve the native desert plants on the site. More than 7,000 of the existing saguaros were transplanted, as were 15,000 other cacti and 50 mesquite trees. The architect also created an environment that allows maximum enjoyment of the natural surroundings. Each guest room has a private exterior entrance and a spacious private patio

THE AUSTERE MAJESTY OF THE DESERT PROVIDES THE PERFECT SETTING FOR THE WESTIN LA PALOMA, A 250-ACRE RESORT NESTLED AT THE BASE OF THE SANTA CATALINA MOUNTAINS. "THE WESTIN LA PALOMA IS REGARDED AS ONE OF TUCSON'S GEMS," SAYS NANCY ALLISON, DIRECTOR OF MARKETING COMMUNICATIONS. "LOCAL RESIDENTS BRING THEIR GUESTS, FAMILIES, AND FRIENDS VISITING FROM OUT OF TOWN. IT'S CONSIDERED ONE OF THE LOVELIEST SPOTS IN TUCSON."

or balcony. Each of the 27 guest buildings has its own courtyard area landscaped with saguaros and trailing high-desert ground cover that complement the resort's southwestern mission-revival architectural style. The resort's signature color, La Paloma rose, was suggested by the dusty rose hues of the area's memorable sunsets.

In the fall of 1998, renowned southwestern chef Janos Wilder relocated his nationally acclaimed Janos restaurant to the resort. "We wanted to find a space in a beautiful building that would be close to our customers, offer fabulous views, and associate us with the best. La Paloma fit all those criteria," Wilder says. Capacity varies, with about 140 seats for fine dining, 10 in a private wine room, and 60 in the J Bar. For special events, approximately 100 can also be seated outside.

Dining variety is the spice of life at La Paloma, where hungry guests and visitors have several options in addition to Janos. The Desert Garden Bistro features views of the Santa Catalinas through 30-foot arched windows, and offers entrées ranging from salads to pasta and fine meats. Guests can also swim up to Sabino's, where underwater bar stools provide the perfect perch for enjoying something tall and cool. Sabino's also offers hot dogs, hamburgers, and deli sandwiches. At the Tennis & Health Center, the Courtside Deli serves up sandwiches, salads, fruit plates, and

soft-serve yogurt, while hungry golfers can take advantage of a snack bar conveniently located on the golf course. Even La Paloma's 24-hour room service is specialized for discriminating guests, with orders arriving from the kitchen on a motorized cart equipped with heating and refrigeration units.

La Paloma also offers a range of meeting facilities that can accommodate groups ranging from five to 2,100 people. Its 42,000 square feet of interior meeting space includes an 18,000-square-

foot ballroom (one of the largest in the Southwest), as well as 16 meeting rooms. In addition, diverse outdoor theme areas provide dramatic settings for group functions.

For the future, The Westin La Paloma plans to maintain its reputation as one of the finest resort destinations in the country. Says Allison, "Our goal has always been to exceed our guests' expectations by providing outstanding service and facilities as a leader in the tourism industry."

ACCORDING TO *GOLF DIGEST*, THE JACK NICKLAUS GOLF COURSE AT LA PALOMA IS ONE OF THE TOP 75 RESORT COURSES IN THE COUNTRY AND ONE OF THE TOP 10 COURSES IN ARIZONA. IN ADDITION, *GOLF*, *GOLF FOR WOMEN*, *GOLFWEEK*, AND *GOLF RESORT GUIDE* ALL RECOGNIZE THE COURSE AS ONE OF THE BEST IN THE COUNTRY, AND *GOLF SHOP OPERATIONS* HAS EVEN RANKED THE LA PALOMA GOLF SHOP AS ONE OF THE TOP 100 IN THE COUNTRY.

OWNED BY CAESAR PARK HOTELS & RESORTS, INC., A SUBSIDIARY OF AOKI CORPORATION, AND MANAGED BY WESTIN HOTELS AND RESORTS, THE 487-ROOM LUXURY RESORT COMBINES SPACIOUS CONFERENCE AND BANQUET FACILITIES WITH A 27-HOLE, JACK NICKLAUS SIGNATURE GOLF COURSE; TENNIS AND RACQUETBALL COURTS; SWIMMING POOLS; A 177-FOOT WATER SLIDE; THREE SPAS; A SWIM-UP BAR; AND A COMPLETE HEALTH CLUB.

© JAMES RANDKLEV

INTERTECH ARCHITECTURAL INTERIORS, INC.	1987	NEW WORLD HOMES	1992
RIGHTFAX, INC.	1987	OPTO POWER CORPORATION	1992
UNIVERSAL AVIONICS SYSTEMS CORPORATION	1988	STARR PASS	1992
STAFFINGSOLUTIONS	1989	THE TUCSON MALL	1992
CONVERGYS CORPORATION	1990	APPLIED INTEGRATION CORPORATION	1993
GREATER TUCSON ECONOMIC COUNCIL	1990	INDUSTRIAL & FINANCIAL SYSTEMS	1996
WEISER LOCK	1990	HAMPTON INN NORTH	1997
PULTE HOME CORPORATION	1991	KWBA-TV58	1998

Ψ INTERTECH ARCHITECTURAL INTERIORS, INC.

INTERTECH ARCHITECTURAL INTERIORS, INC. SPECIALIZES IN A VARIETY OF ARCHITECTURAL PROJECTS, FROM TENANT IMPROVEMENTS TO ENTIRE BUILDING DESIGNS. "OUR ABILITY TO PRODUCE QUALITY DESIGNS FOR ANY BUSINESS WITHIN BUDGET IS ONE OF THE COMPANY'S

INTERTECH ARCHITECTURAL INTERIORS, INC. IS THE MAIN DESIGN FIRM FOR SEVERAL LOCAL OFFICE BUILDINGS, INCLUDING A CONCEPTUAL, THREE-STORY FACILITY IN THE HEART OF WILLIAMS CENTRE IN TUCSON.

strengths," says Wayne Swan, president of the firm. "We design from the inside out, specifically for the user's needs. We are focused on creatively designing the work space to adequately fall within the appropriate budget."

Founded in 1987, Intertech has designed for companies around the United States and the world, with many repeat clients, including Alphagraphics, Inc., Kmart, Davis-Monthan Air Force Base, Brooks Fiber Communications, National Semiconductor, Rincon Research Corporation, Science Applications International Corporation, Charter Funding, Fennemore Craig, Waterfall Economidis, Tucson Police Department, Pima Community College, and the American Consulate in Mexico, as well as several commercial real estate firms. The company has a great deal of experience in retail facilities, restaurants, gas stations, law offices, corporate offices, and medical facilities. It grosses about $500,000 annually, handling approximately 20 percent of the interior office planning in Tucson.

DIVERSITY IN DESIGN

The company is the main interior design firm for several local office buildings, including the Williams Centre, the Plaza

at 5151 East Broadway, Corporate Center Broadway, Centre East, Tucson Office Plaza, Tri-Pointe Plaza, Intergroup of Arizona, Inc., St. Joseph's Medical Plaza, and the downtown Bank of America Plaza.

Intertech's projects have included a dentist's office in Plaza Palomino, designed with screened examining areas, soft lighting, wood trim, and neutral colors, making the office warm and inviting. At the Plaza at 5151 East Broadway, Intertech created an outdoor plaza meant to feel like an atrium, with cascading water and stone sculptures. For the headquarters of the Central Arizona Project in Phoenix, Intertech renovated the organization's large electronic map

of the state canal system, along with new offices and reception area.

"We're designing to our clients' needs," Swan says. Some of Intertech's most recent work includes Dannenberg's Restaurant Bar and Grille, Smith Barney offices, the law offices of Fennemore Craig in Tucson, and multiple temporary processing facilities in Mexico.

"We have a wide variety of projects, therefore we're really good at designing in multiple styles that apply to different buildings," says designer Misti Weaver. At the firm's office, located in the Old Farm Business Park, about a dozen employees work together in an open office designed by Intertech to promote teamwork and design at all levels, both interior and exterior. "We have fun with the teams, which promotes quality design. We use the best individual ideas from team discussions," adds Weaver.

The firm has received several architectural awards and acknowledgements for its designs. Swan is also a member of the City of Tucson Building Code Committee. In addition, Intertech volunteers its services each year to nonprofit organizations in the Tucson area. In 1999, the firm provided preliminary interior design for the Volunteer Center of Tucson.

Swan believes Intertech will continue to concentrate on commercial office and retail environments, and he aims to keep the staff small in order to keep his focus on design rather than management. Offering innovative designs and creative solutions for its clients, Intertech will be a major part of Tucson's design community for many years to come.

THE VIBRANT PALETTE OF COLORS AND THE CUSTOM CREATIVE DESIGN APPLIED TO DR. BLASE'S DENTAL OFFICE ENHANCE THE FUN ATMOSPHERE GEARED TOWARD THE YOUNG PATIENTS HE TREATS.

BRADLEY H. FEDER AND JOSEPH CRACCHIOLO, COFOUNDERS OF RIGHTFAX, INC., HAVE RIDDEN A WAVE OF SKILL AND GOOD FORTUNE TO THE TOP OF THEIR INDUSTRY. ■ SHORTLY AFTER GRADUATING FROM THE UNIVERSITY OF ARIZONA, FEDER AND

Cracchiolo were asked by a Phoenix law firm to devise an efficient way for the company to handle overseas faxing of 300-page documents. The two men took the assignment and pooled their talents to create the software that is the basis of today's RightFAX fax server software.

"Half of business is having the knowledge and sense to take advantage of an opportunity when it comes by," says Cracchiolo, senior vice president of research and development. "The other half is luck." Soon after developing a solution for the law firm, other companies swamped the two men with requests to fax more efficiently.

After founding their company in 1987 to offer network consulting services, Feder and Cracchiolo watched it fast become one of the world's leading developers of advanced network fax server solutions. To meet the demand for faster, more efficient, and less expensive faxing, the company developed a line of products that serves midsize businesses to large, enterprise organizations in more than 45 countries worldwide. In fact, RightFAX software is used in more than 80 percent of Fortune 100 companies and was

named the number one Windows NT fax server in the world by International Data Corporation, a leading computer research analyst.

Privately held until 1996, RightFAX now operates as AVT RightFAX Software Group, a subsidiary of AVT (formerly Applied Voice Technology), which is publicly traded (Nasdaq:AVTC). With headquarters in Kirkland, Washington, AVT develops and markets a line of unified messaging applications. Today, RightFAX employs more than 150 people at its international headquarters in Tucson. RightFAX sells through a channel of approximately 2,100 resellers and distributors worldwide. Its customers include Citibank, American Express, Toyota, Ryder, the U.S. Army, the Disney Company, and Office Depot.

RightFAX associates are enthusiastic, giving 100 percent back to the company that employs them. People work hard, but they are well rewarded. Perks include video games, massages, an annual trip for the top sales associates and departmental employees of the year, and a round of social events ranging from happy hours to a citywide treasure hunt.

RightFAX is proud to give back to its community. The company partners with the American Red Cross to sponsor an annual blood drive, has sent a child to camp through the American Diabetes Association, given holiday gifts to local families through the Salvation Army, and sponsored fund-raising events for the Brewster Center and the Ara Parseghian Foundation. Plus, the company partners with the University of Arizona to review student-written business plans and offer internships. In addition, the firm's cofounders donate their time to lead seminars.

For four years, RightFAX has been named one of the 50 fastest-growing high-tech companies in Arizona. A competition sponsored by Ernst & Young, *USA Today*, and Nasdaq named Cracchiolo and Feder Entrepreneurs of the Year in 1996. In recent years, RightFAX has won more awards than all its competitors combined.

Under the leadership of Cracchiolo and Feder, RightFAX plans to continue innovating, just as it has in the past. Says Cracchiolo, "We will do everything we can to stay at the top."

JOSEPH CRACCHIOLO, COFOUNDER AND SENIOR VICE PRESIDENT OF RESEARCH AND DEVELOPMENT; JULI HOWARD, SENIOR VICE PRESIDENT OF SALES AND MARKETING; AND BRADLEY H. FEDER, COFOUNDER AND PRESIDENT, REPRESENTED THEIR COMPANY AT THE 1998 RIGHTFAX WORLDWIDE PARTNER SUMMIT IN TUCSON.

TOOLS TO HELP PILOTS FLY HAVE HELPED UNIVERSAL AVIONICS SYSTEMS CORPORATION WING ITS WAY TO THE TOP OF THE FLIGHT ELECTRONICS INDUSTRY," SAYS CHARLES H. EDMONDSON, EXECUTIVE VICE PRESIDENT OF THE COMPANY THAT MAKES AND

markets flight management systems. Universal Avionics' high-tech systems and products have been installed on corporate and commercial aircraft around the world.

The company was originally established in Torrance, California, in 1981 with the goal of designing and developing the first flight management system for the corporate and commercial aviation marketplace. The details of a master navigation system had been sketched out several years earlier by Hubert L. Naimer, founder and president of Universal Avionics. An experienced pilot himself, Naimer desired a system that would be capable of accepting input from sources ranging from radio navigation networks to air data information. "He needed and wanted better navigation for his worldwide trips," Edmondson says.

REVOLUTIONIZING FLIGHT
In 1982, Naimer and his team developed the UNS-1 master navigation system, and it revolutionized the flight world. The system integrated these diverse inputs into a single management computer with a pilot-friendly control/display unit in the cockpit. "UNS" is an acronym for universal navigation system, while "1" reinforces the system's role as a single focal point for control of all navigation functions.

The UNS-1 flight management system has evolved over the years with the changing needs of the flight industry. New UNS-1 models have global positioning system receivers that use satellites for navigation, and they have a data link interface for air-to-ground communications. Other Universal Avionics products include cabin information/entertainment systems and cockpit voice recorders. "The flight management system has become the heart of the avionics suite in an aircraft," Edmondson says. "Today, we're recognized as number one as far as flight management systems are concerned."

MOVING TO TUCSON
In 1988, Universal Avionics' marketing and product support groups moved from California to Tucson. Subsequently, sales rose, and the company expanded its Tucson facility from 15,000 to 41,000 square feet. A new 58,000-square-foot manufacturing building, which opened in May 1999, features the latest in engineering and manufacturing techniques. The facility includes state-of-the-art robotics to produce circuit boards that use fine pitch layouts and very small chip-sized components. The new plant also includes a clean room and avionics environmental testing chambers.

Tucson has given Universal Avionics a steady supply of technicians and management-level workers. In addition, Edmondson notes, "City government has been very good to work with." A

graduate of the University of Arizona, Edmondson was pleased to return to the area. "Tucson's climate is beautiful," he says. "Our employees have fallen in love with it. They can afford to live here, and we can support their quality of life by paying them comparable wages."

Universal Avionics has been recognized as one of Arizona's top 50 fastest-growing high technology companies, receiving the AzTech Award in 1996, 1997, and 1998. In addition, Universal Avionics won the Accelerator Award for 1998. The company has plans to provide several new avionics components in addition to their flight management systems and intends to add 100 employees through 1999. Edmondson notes, "The company continues to be recognized as a developer and manufacturer of the latest technology in the avionics industry."

CLOCKWISE FROM TOP:
UNIVERSAL AVIONICS SYSTEMS CORPORATION'S STATE-OF-THE-ART TUCSON FACILITY ENCOMPASSES MORE THAN 100,000 SQUARE FEET.

CHARLES H. EDMONDSON, CORPORATE EXECUTIVE VICE PRESIDENT

UNS-1D FLIGHT MANAGEMENT SYSTEM PROVIDES ADVANCED NAVIGATION FOR CORPORATE AND COMMERCIAL AIRCRAFT.

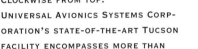

HILE OTHER COMPANIES HAVE A HARD TIME HANDLING LAST-MINUTE CRISES, StaffingSolutions THRIVES ON THEM. ■ A DIVISION OF CAREER BLAZERS, INC., StaffingSolutions IS A TRAINING AND STAFFING

service with offices throughout the United States. The company began business in Tucson in 1989 as Temp Associates and within the first year, had $1 million in sales. The business was then purchased and given its current name in 1995.

"If a business needs people and needs them now, StaffingSolutions will satisfy the requirements to get the number of skilled workers needed," says Roxie Puente, area vice president and general manager of the company. "Our clients are very comfortable with calling us at the last minute," she says. "We're used to putting out fires."

QUALITY SERVICES

StaffingSolutions provides a wide variety of employment options, ranging from light industrial to administrative and clerical work. Puente, who has worked in the temporary employment industry for 22 years, says, "We've even gotten

a call for someone to wear a cactus costume. Another employer needed 120 merchandisers for a grand opening."

Some of the administrative and clerical positions include human resources assistant, administrative assistant, and executive secretary for a variety of companies. In addition, the company also hires workers who are skilled in assembly and production, shipping and receiving, janitorial work, picking and packing, general labor, warehouse work, inventory, and mail clerking. With thousands of temporary workers in the database, StaffingSolutions has a reputation for being able to find large volumes of people. "Our database consists of a variety of people, from students to teachers and even moms," explains Puente.

New applicants are given skills tests, and their references are checked. Those applying for the light industrial

division go through a prescreening, evaluation, interview, safety and policy orientation, background check, and risk management program. All employees go through a company orientation, after which their names are placed in a database, categorized according to skill.

SATISFIED CLIENTS AND EMPLOYEES

StaffingSolutions respects all employees and treats them with fairness, honesty, and integrity. All workers are encouraged to take advantage of the learning center and résumé workshops offered by the company. StaffingSolutions also visits job sites to make sure they're safe. Understanding the work that needs to be done also helps the company to better prepare its employees. "Happy employees means turnover is low," Puente says.

In order for the agency to stay aware of companies' needs around the clock, StaffingSolutions maintains a 24-hour voice mail system that can be accessed by employers and employees. "We're used to not getting any notice at all," Puente says. "If the job starts that day, we're on the phone within half an hour."

StaffingSolutions strives to be its clients' first choice for staffing needs. The company aims to be an industry leader in partnering programs, responsive and cost-effective services, consultative staffing expertise, and creative staffing solutions.

"IF A BUSINESS NEEDS PEOPLE AND NEEDS THEM NOW, STAFFINGSOLUTIONS WILL SATISFY THE REQUIREMENTS TO GET THE NUMBER OF SKILLED WORKERS NEEDED," SAYS ROXIE PUENTE, AREA VICE PRESIDENT AND GENERAL MANAGER OF THE COMPANY. "WE KEEP TUCSON WORKING."

AT STAFFINGSOLUTIONS, (STANDING) ROBERT DUNN, RUTH DUNN, KISMET HARO, (SEATED) VERONICA ARMENTA, ROXIE PUENTE, AND (NOT SHOWN) MONICA BRICK MAKE THE COMPANY THE FIRST CHOICE FOR ITS CLIENTS' STAFFING NEEDS.

BY HELPING TO CREATE THOUSANDS OF JOBS, THE GREATER TUCSON ECONOMIC COUNCIL (GTEC) HAS BOOSTED TUCSON'S PROSPERITY AND QUALITY OF LIFE. WITH A MISSION OF ATTRACTING AND RETAINING QUALITY JOBS FOR THE TUCSON

area, GTEC helps the public and private sectors to identify economic issues and coordinate and facilitate economic development activities that are critical for the community's financial health. To accomplish this, the optics, information technology, environmental technologies, aerospace, biological, teleservices, and plastics and advanced composite materials industries are targeted for recruitment by GTEC.

These efforts have been very successful. Since 1992, GTEC has helped bring more than 97 new or expanding companies into the region, including many operations of Raytheon Missile Systems, the national headquarters of the Muscular Dystrophy Association, and the headquarters and manufacturing facilities of Universal Avionics. ADE Phase Shift Technologies, Burr Brown Corporation, AlliedSignal, America Online, and Intuit have also recognized Tucson's advantages. These companies have created more than 17,000 direct jobs and more

than 19,000 indirect or induced jobs, and have provided $560 million in direct wages to the area.

Today, more than 320 firms are GTEC private sector members, supporting economic development efforts in the Tucson area. Members' benefits include access to professional and precise data on economic development issues; worldwide exposure through a listing in GTEC's Internet business directory; exposure through a new member listing in the *Progress Tucson* newsletter; exposure to businesses relocating to Tucson through a listing in the *GTEC Business Resource and Membership Directory*; opportunities to serve on selected GTEC task forces; voting rights at the GTEC annual meeting elections; and access to quarterly GTEC Board of Directors meetings.

RECOGNIZING THE ADVANTAGES OF TUCSON

Companies are attracted to Tucson for a variety of reasons. Labor, material, utili-

ties, and a tax environment that benefits technology-driven, capital-intensive firms that are export focused make Tucson among the most economical cities in the United States. A wide range of local- and state-assisted training programs is available to meet the need for skilled employees. In addition, workers' compensation premium rates and unemployment insurance rates are among the lowest in the nation. Many firms have also been attracted to Tucson because of the ability to access and partner in research activities under way at the University of Arizona, thereby creating an opportunity to use Arizona's unlimited tax credit for qualified research and development expenses.

Perhaps, though, Tucson's greatest advantage is its workforce. Greater Tucson's population of more than 845,000 is growing twice as fast as the national average, and the age of the average population is below the national average. Some 80.5 percent of the population has

BY HELPING TO CREATE THOUSANDS OF JOBS, THE GREATER TUCSON ECONOMIC COUNCIL (GTEC) HAS BOOSTED TUCSON'S PROSPERITY AND QUALITY OF LIFE, AND HAS WITNESSED THE EXPORT-BASED INDUSTRY CREATE JOBS AND WEALTH IN THE CITY.

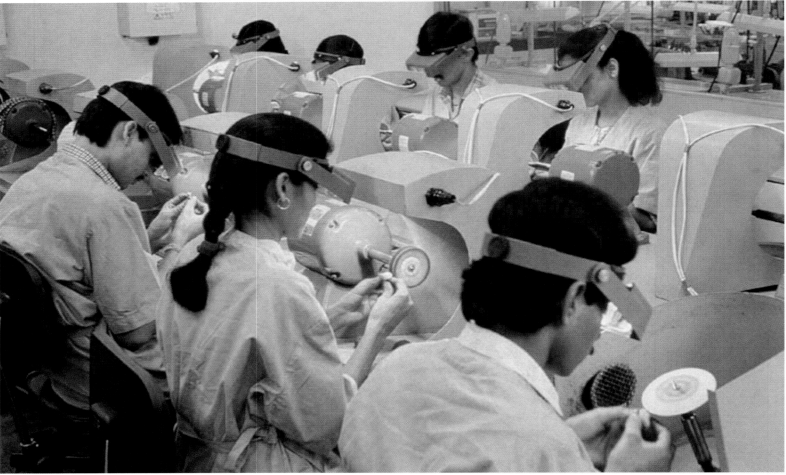

attended school beyond high school (compared to 75 percent nationally), and 23.3 percent of the population has received at least a bachelor's degree.

STRATEGIES FOR SUCCESS

GTEC's Strategic Partnership for Economic Development coordinates with industry representatives, Pima County, Tucson Metropolitan Chamber of Commerce, Tucson Metropolitan Convention and Visitors Bureau, and other agencies. The groups are led by representatives from Tucson's industry clusters, and work together to meet goals and avoid duplication in development efforts.

"The main reason we've been successful in this project is because of cooperation and coordination, pulling together all the players," Robert Gonzales, president and CEO of GTEC says. "Our development efforts have become more efficient and much more successful."

One of the council's key strategies is to build on the model of the industry cluster—a group of related businesses operating in the same geographical area. Tucson is fortunate to have a growing cluster of high-tech companies that create high-paying jobs, and the strategic partnership is actively working to advance this growth through its economic development strategies of business attraction, expansion, and retention.

GTEC's strategies have served as a model for other economic development agencies around the country, and Gonzales often travels to different communities to discuss his agency's success. "There are many areas following the cluster concept, but few have implemented it as successfully as GTEC has," Gonzales says.

More important, however, the strategic partnership annually assembles a legislative agenda, addressing issues such as elimination of the state throwback tax on exports, reduction in corporate income tax rate by 2 percent in two years (down to 7 percent), establishment of an unlimited tax credit for qualified research and development expenses, and progressive investment in workforce development and job training programs.

THE FUTURE OF GTEC

In the future, GTEC wants to find ways to help recent graduates and other residents stay in Tucson and start up their own businesses in the city. "We're going to continue emphasize job creation through business attraction," says Gonzales. "We will also refocus on developing the local industry clusters, the foundations that support the growth and expansion of local cluster business, as well as entrpreneurs.

"We're going to become more involved in facilitating entrepreneurship, and coordinating with Tucson's vast network of experts who can assist start-up companies. In Tucson, we have tremendous opportunity. We want to take advantage of it through education, workforce development, technology transfer, development of a local capital network, and maintaining our exceptional quality of life."

CLUSTERS OF HIGH-TECH INDUSTRIES MAKE TUCSON AN IDEAL SITE FOR RESEARCH AND DEVELOPMENT.

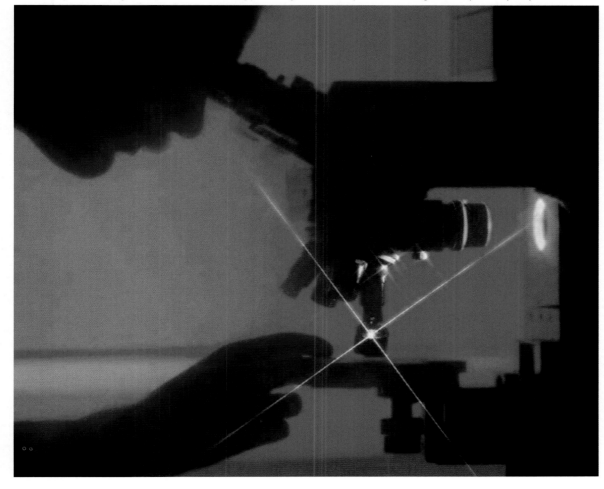

ESTABLISHED IN 1904 AS A FAMILY-OWNED FOUNDRY IN SOUTH GATE, WEISER LOCK® STARTED OUT AS A SPECIALIST IN HARDWARE AND ORNATE, CUSTOM-DESIGNED LOCKS, SOME OF WHICH WERE FEATURED IN FILMS AND USED IN THE HOMES

of movie stars. Today, the success of its technologically innovative products has placed Weiser Lock in second place in the $1 billion-plus lock industry's mid-priced residential segment. The patented Brilliance® Lifetime Anti-Tarnish Finish and the Powerbolt® Electronic Home Access System have ensured Weiser's growth, with new products making up 60 percent of the company's sales, according to Marketing Vice President Dave Sutton.

In 1967, Weiser was purchased by Norris Industries, Inc., which merged with Masco Building Products Corp.® in 1985. Weiser moved from California to Tucson in January 1990, and over the next few years, the company consolidated its corporate offices and manufacturing operations in its 340,000-square-foot administrative and production space in Midvale Park. In Tucson, Weiser has an employee base of about 850 workers, but also maintains offices in Canada and the United Kingdom.

As a subsidiary of Masco Building Products Corp., Weiser Lock has 17 percent growth in a market where average growth is 4 percent. The company's products are offered at home centers and hardware stores throughout North America. "The company's aggressive marketing has helped ensure its success," Sutton says.

BRILLIANCE

Introduced in 1995, the Brilliance finish, offered on all bright brass and chrome exterior hardware, was created by Weiser Lock engineers as a solution to the problem that has always plagued brass: its tendency to tarnish. "We are the only one in the United States with this technology," Sutton says.

Brilliance uses the principle of physical vapor deposition, the same technology NASA uses to protect the space shuttle from burning up during reentry into the Earth's atmosphere. The process involves using an electrical arc

created from a metal electrode inside a vacuum chamber. Gas is then introduced into the chamber. This causes the finishing materials to shoot at the lock sets with great force, providing a finish that's thinner than a human hair, yet stronger than other finishes on the market. There are 22 patents on the process with another 10 pending.

Because it is not a lacquer or after-finish application, the bond is essentially inseparable from the product. The Brilliance finish stands up to ultraviolet rays, humidity, extreme cold, and salt spray. The finish even stands up to the year-round strong sunlight in Tucson, Sutton says. The process is environmentally friendly, using no volatile organic compounds and creating few environmental and work safety hazards. It also produces no hazardous or toxic wastes.

Brilliance is the only finish in the field offered on a complete line of exterior products that comes with a full lifetime anti-tarnish warranty. In 1995, Weiser

QUALITY PRODUCTS—SUCH AS THE PRESTIGE™ SERIES AURORA HANDLE-SET (LEFT) AND THE WELCOME HOME™ SERIES VALENCIA LEVER (RIGHT)—ARE WHY WEISER LOCK HOLDS SUCH HIGH RANK IN THE $1 BILLION-PLUS LOCK INDUSTRY'S MIDPRICED RESIDENTIAL SEGMENT.

RICK GAYLE

Lock unveiled the Brilliance finish on its midpriced line of residential door hardware. The company now offers a line of key-entry handlesets, knobsets, leversets, and dead bolts in a bright brass finish, guaranteed to never tarnish, discolor, or corrode.

Weiser Lock introduced a line of Brilliance door accessories in 1998, including kick plates, knockers, numbers, and door viewers, to complement the door hardware already available in the Brilliance finish. The Brilliance finish has also made its way into other areas of the home. Delta Faucet Co. recently unveiled the finish on a line of brass faucets called Innovations. Alsons Corp. has also introduced a line of brass showerheads that feature Brilliance. Both companies are divisions of Masco Corp. "The advantages of the Brilliance finish encourage consumers to pay a little more money and get a lot more for it," Sutton says.

POWERBOLT HOME ACCESS SYSTEMS

Brilliance is also offered on Weiser Lock's Powerbolt 1000 Electronic Keyless Home Access System, a code-accessed locking and entry system with a mechanical key-entry backup. The Powerbolt provides quick entry for home owners and their

families with a four- to eight-digit access code. When people leave a home, they can lock up using a one-touch locking button. Each Powerbolt includes a heavy-duty deadbolt for maximum security and requires no wiring, just four AA batteries. The system can store two programmable codes, and service personnel such as painters, baby-sitters, and house cleaners can be given a temporary access code that can be changed easily and as often as necessary. The system also includes a built-in automatic code-break alarm system, which is triggered when incorrect numbers are entered. "This is the first time such products have been available for midpriced residential markets," Sutton says.

Through a joint venture with the Chamberlain® Group, Inc., of Elmhurst, Illinois, the world's largest manufacturer of residential garage door openers, Weiser Lock has also developed the Powerbolt 3000 Home Access System, the world's first radio frequency, remote control entry system. The system lets the operator lock or unlock a home from the safety of a car with the touch of a button. Audible and visual indicators confirm that doors are properly locked or unlocked.

The Powerbolt 3000 Home Access System includes Security+™ Anti-Theft Coding. Each time a system remote is

activated, the code automatically rolls over to any one of 100 billion new codes, never to be repeated. This defends against burglars with code-grabbing devices. The electronic deadbolt also includes a low-battery indicator. Small enough to carry in a pocket or purse, this is the first remote control that connects a home owner's door locks, garage-door opener, and interior lighting systems. No wiring is necessary for the system. The electronic dead bolt can be installed in standard door preparations. Weiser offers a lifetime warranty on all mechanical components and a one-year limited warranty on electrical components.

The Powerbolt's link with garage doors and lighting systems was made possible through a joint development agreement with the Chamberlain Group. The Powerbolt 3000 Home Access System remote will operate all garage-door openers with Security+ Anti-Theft Coding by Chamberlain, Lift-Master®, and Sears Craftsman®. Other garage-door openers require the Powerbolt 3000 Remote Garage Door Opener module. The Powerbolt remote system is also compatible with the HomeLink® Universal Transmitter, made by Prince Corp., a division of Johnson Controls®, which makes interior trim and electronics for the global automotive industry. "The new radio frequency,

PROVIDING QUICK HOME ENTRY, CONVENIENCE, AND PEACE OF MIND, THE POWERBOLT® 3000 SYSTEM REMOTE AND ELECTRONIC DEADBOLT (LEFT) AND THE POWERBOLT® 1000 TOUCHPAD ELECTRONIC DEADBOLT (RIGHT) ARE AVAILABLE FOR THE MIDPRICED RESIDENTIAL MARKET.

THE WELCOME HOME™ SERIES IS
WEISER'S LARGEST CATEGORY, OFFER-
ING HIGH-QUALITY PRODUCTS IN A WIDE
VARIETY OF STYLES AND FINISHES, SUCH
AS THE AUGUSTA ENTRYSET.

remote control Powerbolt 3000 gives the home owner unparalleled convenience and peace of mind through its compatible links with other technologically innovative leaders," Sutton says.

BUILDING PARTNERSHIPS

Weiser's ability to attract such partners as Chamberlain and the Prince Corp., coupled with the backing of its parent company, Masco, demonstrates the company's growing power and influence in the residential door hardware field. The increasing demand for Weiser Lock products has been recognized by Lowe's® Home Centers, which named Weiser Lowe's Hardware Division Vendor of the Year in 1995 and 1997.

TRADITIONAL DOOR HARDWARE

Weiser offers three categories of traditional door hardware to meet differing consumer needs. The Prestige™ series is an elegant yet affordable line of solid brass hardware consisting of handlesets, entrysets, and dead bolts for exterior doors, as well as leversets and knobsets for interior doors. The line includes three style families: the contemporary Colonnade group, the graceful and elegant Aurora family, and the Acacia collection, a formal, European-influenced look. The Welcome Home™ series is Weiser's largest category, offering high-quality products in a wide variety of styles and finishes at popular price points. Weiser also manufactures the Basics™ series of products positioned to introduce price conscious consumers to Weiser Lock quality and durability.

Weiser Lock also focuses significant resources on residential new construction markets. Sales and marketing professionals develop relationships with small and large builders to help ensure the placement of Weiser products in hundreds of new housing developments each year. "With the building boom, Weiser can't make enough doorknobs," Sutton says.

In the future, Weiser plans to expand its electronics line, developing home security systems that will allow home owners to check on their homes via satellite or the Internet. Also in the works is an update of Weiser's lever offering. Levers are currently the fastest-growing product category in the door hardware industry. "We're doing a lot of things to keep up," Sutton says.

WEISER LOCK'S WELCOME HOME SERIES
OFFERS THE PHOENIX KNOBSET (LEFT).

THE PRESTIGE™ SERIES IS AN ELEGANT
LINE OF SOLID BRASS HARDWARE FEA-
TURING THREE STYLE FAMILIES. THE
ACACIA COLLECTION (RIGHT) IS A FOR-
MAL, EUROPEAN-INFLUENCED LOOK,
WHILE THE COLONNADE GROUP IS
MORE CONTEMPORARY (MIDDLE).

ROVIDING INTEGRATED CUSTOMER CARE AND BILLING SERVICES, CONVERGYS CORPORATION HELPS COMPANIES TRANSFORM THEIR CUSTOMER RELATIONSHIPS INTO A COMPETITIVE ADVANTAGE. LED BY PRESIDENT AND CHIEF EXECUTIVE OFFICER JAMES F. ORR,

Convergys provides call center solutions to marketing-intensive companies worldwide. Its services include communications, technology, financial services, consumer products, and direct-response marketing firms.

In Tucson, Convergys runs a customer support call center. The local Convergys Customer Management Group provides and manages customer support solutions for companies worldwide in lead generation, customer service, technical support, and customer acquisition and retention. Convergys aims to help companies gain greater customer loyalty, reduce costs, drive innovation, and increase revenue.

MAKING THE MOST OF CUSTOMER RELATIONSHIPS

Convergys acts as an extension of its clients' businesses. Its billing and customer care management programs help the companies make the most of their customer relationships. Convergys clients make connections that are more profitable with their customers and employees, spurring overall growth and satisfaction. Billing and customer information is key to a provider's ability to serve customers. Convergys offers communications carriers

and utility companies reliability, skill, industry knowledge, and state-of-the-art data and call centers.

The company's services also include customer and information management; dealer referral programs; billing solutions; bill stream consolidation; switch management; employee care services; service order and traffic processing; receivables management; business-to-business telesales account management; credit assessment and collections; customer targeting and acquisition; market research and customer value management; interactive billing technology; database marketing services; service setup, provision, and pricing; interactive customer services, including Internet technology; and usage processing.

The company's applications include billing for single or multiple services, which allows a single view of customer/single-invoice strategies, as well as package pricing and billing for multiple services; and service/network element provisioning, which allocates network-based resources and services to a customer, and provides user-friendly interfaces and automation to allow quick provisioning of new services. Convergys applications also provide for

new service plans, and allow new pricing plans to be created and existing plans to be modified.

INCREASING REVENUES

With 33,000 employees serving markets that include the United States, Canada, the United Kingdom, and Europe, the company handles more than 1 million calls each day. Convergys also handles more than 1 million bills every day, including about 30 percent of all U.S. wireless subscribers. In 1998, revenues for the Cincinnati-based Convergys reached $1.45 billion, and the company reported record second quarter financial results for the three months ending June 30, 1999.

The company also has received several honors and awards, including an award of excellence in on-line technical communication from the Society for Technical Communication for the company's computer-based training.

"I am encouraged by the progress we have made on our strategy for growth and the continued expansion of our core business," Orr says. "Beyond delivering positive financial results, both of our operating units continue to add industry-leading clients in high-growth segments."

THE LOCAL CONVERGYS CUSTOMER MANAGEMENT GROUP PROVIDES AND MANAGES CUSTOMER SUPPORT SOLUTIONS FOR COMPANIES WORLDWIDE IN LEAD GENERATION, CUSTOMER SERVICE, TECHNICAL SUPPORT, AND CUSTOMER ACQUISITION AND RETENTION.

WHEN LOOKING FOR A HOME IN TUCSON, HOME BUYERS NEED LOOK NO FURTHER THAN THE COMMUNITIES OFFERED BY PULTE HOME CORPORATION. WHETHER IT'S RETREAT AT THE BLUFFS, REFLECTIONS AT THE BLUFFS, Canción del Sol, or one of the several other communities in the Greater Tucson area, buyers are sure to find what they're looking for.

"Whether you are a move-down buyer or a first-time buyer, Pulte has a community developed with you in mind," says Andy Pedersen, manager of strategic marketing for Pulte.

◄ CHRIS MOONEY, BALFOUR WALKER STUDIOS

MEETING CUSTOMERS' NEEDS

Established in Tucson in 1991, Pulte has performed extensive research to find out what people want and need in a house, and as a result, offers a wide range of home styles and floor plans. Because many of the floor plans are flexible, buyers can make changes based on their needs. Pulte also offers an extensive list of options ranging from paint color to a choice of tile styles. Prompted by consumer demand, Pulte has made a point of including more storage space, even in its smaller homes. "We spend a great deal of time researching what people want," Pedersen says. "The exciting thing is being able to provide them with what they didn't expect to find."

Pulte customers stay informed during the building process through periodic meetings with the salesperson, building superintendent, and customer care representative. The company continues to care for its customers even after they've moved in: The Pulte Protection Plan guarantees the quality of the house for 10 years, and the company's customer care department helps answer people's questions about their new homes.

Preserving the character of the desert is also important to Pulte. In the Bluffs community, Pulte left 60 acres of open, cactus-filled desert between its upper and lower developments. "Families in those neighborhoods have their own private nature trail," says Pedersen. "It helps the community feel better."

Pulte Home Corporation goes to great lengths to ensure its homes are energy efficient, and participates in the Energy Star program with the U.S. Department of Energy and the Environmental Protection Agency. Heating and cooling costs are guaranteed at the Retreat at the Bluffs, and if those numbers are exceeded, GreenStone, a Louisiana-Pacific company, will pay the difference. "We've realized this program is important," Pedersen says, "especially for first-time buyers. Even though we're spending money up front, the home owner will save money in the long run."

BUILDING COMMUNITIES

Based in Bloomfield Hills, Michigan, Pulte Home Corporation was founded in 1954 by William J. Pulte, chairman of the board of directors. With divisions around the United States, the company was ranked the nation's number-one builder in 1999 by *Professional Builder* magazine. It had more than 20,000 total new residential closings in 1998, when its total housing revenue topped $2.9 billion.

Pulte's employees have a stellar track record in both sales and customer service. The Tucson division was awarded the company's Peak Performance Award in 1998, ranking among the top five for customer satisfaction of all its divisions nationwide.

"Envisioning a community takes time," says Pedersen. "We plan the specifics of a new community at least two years before we start selling." It's this attention to detail and to the needs of its customers that ensures that Pulte will be helping to build a growing Tucson for many years to come.

◄ CHRIS MOONEY, BALFOUR WALKER STUDIOS

PULTE HOME CORPORATION'S ATTENTION TO DETAIL AND TO THE NEEDS OF ITS CUSTOMERS ENSURES THAT IT WILL BE HELPING TO BUILD A GROWING TUCSON FOR MANY YEARS TO COME (TOP).

PULTE OFFERS A WIDE RANGE OF HOME STYLES AND FLOOR PLANS. BECAUSE MANY OF THE FLOOR PLANS ARE FLEXIBLE, BUYERS CAN MAKE CHANGES BASED ON THEIR NEEDS (BOTTOM).

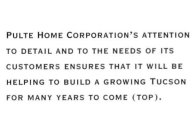

 PTO POWER CORPORATION DESIGNS AND MANUFACTURES HIGH-POWER SEMICONDUCTOR LASERS. THESE SMALL "LIGHT-BULBS ON A CHIP" EMIT LARGE AMOUNTS OF LASER LIGHT AND ENABLE A RANGE OF APPLICATIONS WHERE HIGHLY

controlled spots of heat are required.

Producing high-performance products complemented by strong customer support and enabling pricing, Opto Power's mission is to enable and expand the use of high-power diode lasers for a variety of telecommunication, medical, materials processing, graphics, and illumination applications. Opto Power's products range in output power from about one watt to hundreds and even thousands of watts. Most products are available as fiber-coupled units. Optical fibers allow the emitted light to be directed to remote locations as required for the application.

Because Opto Power is a vertically integrated manufacturer, the company can custom-design lasers for specific original equipment manufacturer (OEM) applications. In addition, Opto Power Corporation is a Spectra-Physics Lasers, Inc. company. Spectra-Physics manufactures and distributes lasers and laser systems, with sales, service, and support located in more than 35 countries.

HIGH-TECH SOLUTIONS

Diode lasers have a high electrical-to-optical power conversion efficiency and can deliver high-quality light for a variety of applications. Diodes produce light with far less power consumption, cost, and bulk than that associated with other laser and non-laser sources.

Opto Power's rapid growth is a result of its large-scale production men-

tality, proprietary manufacturing processes, and emphasis on quality and affordable pricing. All aspects of production are in-house, including epitaxy, processing, packaging, assembly, fiber coupling, testing, and burn-in.

For many years, Opto Power has held world records for the highest-output power for a variety of device configurations.

The company owns its 78,000-square-foot facility near Tucson's international airport. Employing approximately 180 people, Opto Power is proud to be a good corporate citizen of Tucson and encourages its employees to personally support worthwhile community activities.

CLOCKWISE FROM TOP: OPTO POWER CORPORATION DESIGNS AND MANUFACTURES HIGH-POWER SEMICONDUCTOR LASERS. THESE SMALL "LIGHT-BULBS ON A CHIP" EMIT LARGE AMOUNTS OF LASER LIGHT AND ENABLE A RANGE OF APPLICATIONS WHERE HIGHLY CONTROLLED SPOTS OF HEAT ARE REQUIRED.

DIODE LASERS HAVE A HIGH ELECTRICAL-TO-OPTICAL POWER CONVERSION EFFICIENCY AND CAN DELIVER HIGH-QUALITY FOR THERMAL APPLICATIONS.

EMPLOYING APPROXIMATELY 180 PEOPLE, OPTO POWER IS PROUD TO BE A GOOD CORPORATE CITIZEN OF TUCSON AND ENCOURAGES ITS EMPLOYEES TO PERSONALLY SUPPORT WORTHWHILE COMMUNITY ACTIVITIES.

H

ELPING PEOPLE LIVE OUT THEIR DREAMS IS WHAT WE ARE ALL ABOUT," SAYS NEW WORLD HOMES FOUNDER AND PRESIDENT LAWRENCE C. LEUNG. ■ NEW WORLD HOMES WAS FOUNDED BY LEUNG IN 1992. TODAY, IT HAS GROWN INTO ONE OF THE TOP

home-building companies in the city, having developed 16 planned communities in and around Tucson. The company is focused not only on developing and building homes, but also on establishing relationships.

"Purchasing a new home can be a scary proposition. We pride ourselves on assisting the prospective buyer through the entire process," states Leung. "Whether it is the drafting of a purchase contract, assisting with finances, choosing carpet samples, or explaining how to work the air-conditioning, our staff is trained to make the home-buying experience pleasurable." This commitment to the home buyer has paid off because many customers have bought their second and third homes from New World.

New World's homes are generally detached, single-family houses that range in size from 1,000 to 2,600 square feet, and in price from $90,000 to $140,000, including the lots.

NEW WORLD HOMES PRODUCES HOMES, SUCH AS ITS MODEL 1004 MONTERRA (TOP) AND MODEL 1002 MONTERRA (BOTTOM), THAT INCORPORATE MANY ELEMENTS OF SOUTHWESTERN CULTURE, AS WELL AS THE BEAUTY AND SERENITY OF THE DESERT ENVIRONMENT.

BUILDING HOMES IN TUCSON

"Tucson is a very unique place," says Leung, who moved here from his native Hong Kong in 1970 to chase the American dream. "It has the charm of a small town, but we have the amenities of a big city—not to mention the year-round warmth."

After attending the University of Arizona, Leung got a pharmacy degree in 1974 with the intent of continuing on to medical school, but he decided to go into business instead. He started as a real estate broker and expanded into land development, planning, and zoning, prior to establishing New World Homes.

"I fell in love with Tucson," says Leung, whose planned communities include Rancho Escondido, Mona Lisa Heights, La Cholla Ridge, Suncrest, Wilmot Pointe, Monterra Hills, Casa Del Rio, Mesquite Crest, and The Hills on La Canada.

In a business that has been dominated by national home-building companies, New World has created a niche in providing a quality home that is affordably priced for first-time home buyers, empty nesters, and people moving up for the first time.

Leung is quick to point out that the key to New World's success is its dedicated staff of approximately 25. "I have a very devoted staff," Leung says, which includes his wife of 27 years, Nancy, and son, Michael, who both share his commitment. "I am very fortunate. I have employees who have been with me since the start of the company, and who are devoted to the same goals and commitments that I have."

New World's employees routinely visit sales offices, discussing with prospective home buyers what they want in a new house. "Listening to the customer and providing a quality product

is what has made us successful," says Terry Klinger, senior vice president.

New World pays close attention to the changing lifestyles of its customers. New floor plans are constantly being designed to meet the demands of the customers. Input is sought from sales staff and prospective home buyers before the building process starts. Leung himself walks through homes as they're being built to make sure the plans create comfortable environments. If he recognizes a problem or has an idea, Leung makes changes on the spot to ensure the buyer's satisfaction. "We are building a house that all of us would be proud to live in," exclaims Leung. As a testament to the fact, more than nine members of Leung's staff live in a New World Home.

In addition to the routine walk-through at closing, the company offers an intermediate walk-through while walls are still open so the buyer can ask questions about construction techniques and review the construction process. Also, 90 days after closing, New World offers a final walk-through with warranty and service personnel. The buyer is reacquainted with the operations and management of the home, down to details like changing an air filter or adjusting a water heater.

ENVIRONMENT PRESERVATION

Many people are attracted to the Tucson valley by the beauty and serenity of the desert environment. "It is important to take an environmentally sensitive approach to development, preserving open space and protecting the integrity of the land," says Leung.

Many New World developments are built with special attention focused on the well-being of the environment. An undisturbed natural wash filled with cacti and other plants runs through one of the company's projects, Rancho Escondido.

In order to preserve the wash, New World spent an extra $200,000 to build up the land for the surrounding homes to assure adequate flood control. The alternative was grading the entire area, which would have destroyed the plants growing in the wash. "Aesthetically, it's an asset," Leung says. "We preserved that area and turned it into more of a focal point.

"When we can, we leave as much area as possible in its natural state. We take inventory of all cacti and trees on the site and try to incorporate them into the subdivision. It is important because this is where we live," says Leung.

IN THE LATE 1800s, RICHARD STARR ONCE RAN STAGECOACH TOURS THROUGH STARR PASS IN THE RUGGED TUCSON MOUNTAINS, GIVING VISITORS AN OPPORTUNITY TO VISIT THE WILDS OF WESTERN TUCSON. ONE HUNDRED YEARS LATER, SIGNATURE PROPERTIES HAS

developed this historic pass along with 1,400 acres, giving visitors to Tucson access to a premier, master-planned resort residential community, Starr Pass.

Starr Pass offers a wide range of residential and resort living. The residential environment is as diverse as the natural environment, with maintenance-free homes ranging from $150,000 to $2 million, custom homes estates lining the perimeter of the championship golf complex.

Placed apart from the residential community, the Marriott Resort/Convention Hotel is nestled in a box canyon surrounded by Tucson Mountain Park, yet highly elevated for spectacular city lights views. Guests at the 575-room hotel can take advantage of the traditional resort amenities: 36 holes of desert golf with the new 18 holes designed by Arnold

Palmer, tennis, swimming, and a separate, 25,000-square-foot luxury spa.

SPLENDOR OF NATURE

Guests can enjoy the splendor of nature unique to this resort on many hiking, biking, and horseback riding trails within the 22,000-acre park, and an interpretation center is planned to educate visitors on the wonderful world of nature in the Sonoran Desert.

It is not uncommon for area residents and visitors to encounter deer, coyotes, roadrunners, javelinas, bobcats, rabbit, quail, or the resident mountain lion going into his cave. The Sonoran Desert's magnificent vegetation, especially the giant saguaro cactus, is abundant throughout Starr Pass and Tucson Mountain Park.

Starr Pass is honored to have won several state and national awards for its

efforts in preservation and revegetation throughout the development, including the National Improvement Award of Merit for improving the environment for all mankind, and for promoting, protecting, and preserving the heritage of beauty for all future generations.

When the day is done, the brilliantly colored, reflective sunsets and the stars provide the views of choice. Under the watchful eye of the Kitt Peak Observatory, all lights in Starr Pass are dimmed, to the delight of planetary observers.

THE MEANING OF LOCATION

Most residents purchase homes at Starr Pass because of the location. However, the meaning of location varies with each person you ask. Some say it is the views from Starr Pass, 300 feet above the city lights, which sparkle like candles. To others, it is the quiet of the mountain parks interrupted only by the howl of coyotes or the songs of the most varied of species of wild birds. For businesspeople, it is the five-minute drive to downtown Tucson—the professional and cultural center of the city—or the 15-minute ride to the airport, which provides them easy access to wherever they need to go.

To some, location is the feeling of the golf course below your backyard, which gives a home owner a sense of serenity. The initial Starr Pass 18-hole course was developed as a Tournament Players Club (TPC) Championship course, where several professional and amateur events are held. Arnold Palmer and Ed Seay will improve on this excellent golf experience by creating an additional 18 holes of resort play utilizing the natural topography of the mountains and washes running through the property.

For all, traveling into Starr Pass is like entering a new world, a world of peace and quiet with abundant nature, where the quality of life is measured in the sounds of relaxation and recreation. Starr Pass is a place where one visit can last a lifetime.

THE DESERT LABORATORY

One hundred years ago, Richard Starr was not the only one who embraced this magnificent location. The Carnegie Foundation established the Desert Laboratory in the late 1800s to study the ecology of

THE STARR PASS RESIDENTIAL ENVIRONMENT IS AS DIVERSE AS THE NATURAL ENVIRONMENT, WITH MAINTENANCE-FREE HOMES RANGING FROM $150,000 TO $2 MILLION, CUSTOM HOMES ESTATES (TOP).

IN THE LATE 1800s, RICHARD STARR ONCE RAN STAGECOACH TOURS THROUGH STARR PASS IN THE RUGGED TUCSON MOUNTAINS, GIVING VISITORS AN OPPORTUNITY TO VISIT THE WILDS OF WESTERN TUCSON. ONE HUNDRED YEARS LATER, SIGNATURE PROPERTIES HAS DEVELOPED THIS HISTORIC PASS AS A PREMIER, MASTER-PLANNED RESORT RESIDENTIAL COMMUNITY (BOTTOM).

CLOCKWISE FROM TOP LEFT:
IT IS NOT UNCOMMON FOR AREA RESI-
DENTS AND VISITORS TO ENCOUNTER
DEER AMONG THE SONORAN DESERT'S
MAGNIFICENT VEGETATION, WHICH IS
ABUNDANT THROUGHOUT STARR PASS
AND TUCSON MOUNTAIN PARK.

THE STARR PASS 18-HOLE GOLF COURSE
WAS DEVELOPED AS A TOURNAMENT
PLAYERS CLUB (TPC) CHAMPIONSHIP
COURSE, WHERE SEVERAL PROFESSIONAL
AND AMATEUR EVENTS ARE HELD.

WHEN THE DAY IS DONE, THE STARS
AND SKY ABOVE TUCSON PROVIDE THE
VIEWS OF CHOICE. UNDER THE WATCHFUL
EYE OF THE KITT PEAK OBSERVATORY,
ALL LIGHTS IN STARR PASS ARE DIMMED,
TO THE DELIGHT OF PLANETARY
OBSERVERS.

the Sonoran Desert. In the mid 1950s, the University of Arizona continued that research, and today the Desert Laboratory on Tumamoc Hill is the oldest research project in the world. The integrity of this most important research has now been assured with the signing of the development agreement between Pima County and Signature Properties.

By working together with the University of Arizona, neighborhood communities, and many other local environmental groups, Starr Pass is assuring that several wildlife corridors connect the Desert Laboratory to the Tucson Mountains through Starr Pass. This vital linkage, where the wildlife can roam freely between the laboratory

and the Tucson Mountain Park, will be an on-site laboratory to study the ecology of the Sonoran Desert for years to come. Starr Pass is dedicated to honoring those who have come before, and to reaching out and making every effort to ensure animals, plants, and humans can live together in harmony into the future.

APPLIED INTEGRATION CORPORATION ENVISIONS WHERE TECHNOLOGY IS HEADED AND DEVELOPS PRODUCTS WITH THE FUTURE IN MIND. THE COMPANY IS A LEADER IN THE DEVELOPMENT OF INNOVATIVE ELECTRONIC COMPUTER-

and communications-related products, including optics, imaging, motion systems, interferometry, wireless communications, and signal processing.

In addition to its current products and services, Applied Integration designs and manufactures custom products, alters existing products, and develops software to meet the unique needs of a particular application. It specializes in computers and peripherals that provide wireless communications, video mastering, authoring, routing, switching, and distribution. The sole developer and only manufacturer of in-system video switching and routing interface peripherals, Applied Integration plans to release a security surveillance control system with features such as a motion detection alarm, a digital video data compressor to maximize storage space, and intelligent image recording control, which directs the camera image recorder to be started and stopped by user-defined events. This eliminates the need for hours of continuous security recording when there is no activity.

CUTTING-EDGE TECHNOLOGY

Founded in 1992, Applied Integration's original mission involved the design and production of video equipment for military surveillance systems, including navy AWACS aircraft and army forward command post communications. The end of the cold war curtailed business, so the company developed a new product line that allowed users to take a single monitor and hook up several cameras to it. This technology led to Applied Integration's development of the ArielNet Wireless Hand Held Communications Terminal.

THE PRINCIPALS OF APPLIED INTEGRATION ARE (FROM LEFT) JEROME DiCENSO, MANUFACTURING ENGINEER AND CORPORATE VICE PRESIDENT; FREDERICK J. PINGAL, FOUNDER, PRESIDENT, AND SENIOR ENGINEER; AND KAREN BOCK, COMPANY DIRECTOR AND CORPORATE OFFICER.

NASA APPROACHED APPLIED INTEGRATION CORPORATION WHEN IT NEEDED A VIDEO SWITCHING DEVICE TO ROUTE ITS PLANNED HIGH-RESOLUTION VIDEO CAMERA IMAGES OF MICROGRAVITY EXPERIMENTS. THESE EXPERIMENTS WILL BE CONDUCTED ABOARD THE JAPAN SCIENCE MODULE (JSM) OF THE PLANNED INTERNATIONAL SPACE STATION. THE APPLIED INTEGRATION VIDEO SWITCH, SPECIALLY DESIGNED AND MANUFACTURED FOR NASA, ROUTES HIGH-RESOLUTION VIDEO IMAGES FROM AS MANY AS 32 VIDEO CAMERAS TO ANY OF 32 DESTINATIONS.

DAVID BEAN PHOTOGRAPHY

With ArielNet, a communications system of wireless, handheld units allows personnel in the field to transmit data remotely to a company's main computer.

Now, Applied Integration supplies similar products for the military as well as the security industry. The InCharge System, for instance, allows people to view security camera input via the Internet on regular personal computers. The computers can be across the hall or around the world. The company is currently developing many more of these functions to go on computer chips, so clients won't need special equipment to view the images. "We invented wireless video networking," says Applied Integration President Frederick Pingal. "This is where we're going: Video on demand over networks and wireless networking."

The company has installed the system in places ranging from gated communities to local banks. One of the company's most innovative products, the InCharge systems provide a range of security. The InCharge System 1000 provides basic on-site monitoring, while System 2000 provides inexpensive remote monitoring for small to medium-sized businesses. System 3000 provides an affordable remote monitoring solution for users who need to store a lot of data. System 4000 provides a wireless system for remote monitoring applications where running wires is impractical. System 5000 is for the customer who requires a large number of inputs and activity detection.

The InCharge System allows users to dial up a remote site and see exactly what is occurring at any time of the day or night. Events can be seen as they occur, with consistent image clarity. Multisite monitoring allows quick reference, and the system logs alarm events, like glass breaking or a smoke detector going

off. Pingal foresees many uses for the InCharge System, like theft prevention for warehouses, supermarkets, and convenience stores, as well as monitoring of patients, children, and the people who care for them. The system can also help people exchange information without being within speaking distance of each other. Instead of traveling to a work site, repair crews, for example, can look at faraway problems, figure out solutions, and then tell workers at the site how to make the necessary repairs. The technology also allows members of law enforcement to be equipped with a personal wireless camera, which can transmit data back to a command center.

CHANGING THE WORLD

Applied Integration is the natural result of Pingal's boyhood fascination with all things mechanical. "When I was born, I knew how the world worked. I was a prodigy in physics," says Pingal. "I built my first radio at eight. At 13, I was fixing all the neighbors' TV sets. My heroes are people like Thomas Edison and Howard Hughes."

Thanks to Pingal's foresight and creativity, the company's technology is out of this world—literally. A Digital Video Crosspoint Switch developed by Applied Integration will be installed on the international space station now under construction hundreds of miles above the Earth. Applied Integration's products will be used to compile input from several cameras around the station.

"To change the world could be fun," says Pingal, and he has made Tucson the home base from which he hopes to make that change. Applied Integration chose Tucson as its headquarters because of its growing importance as an electronic design and manufacturing center. "The vendors are here; the employees are all here. We like to bring the wealth and the knowledge here," says Pingal.

DEVELOPMENT OF NEW PRODUCTS IS ONE OF APPLIED INTEGRATION'S MAIN ACTIVITIES. STATE-OF-THE-ART, COMPUTER-AIDED DESIGN TOOLS PLAY A CRUCIAL ROLE IN ALLOWING THE COMPANY TO SWIFTLY DEPLOY NEW PRODUCTS TO MEET THE RAPIDLY CHANGING NEEDS OF TODAY'S MARKETPLACE.

APPLIED INTEGRATION'S MANUFACTURING FACILITY INCLUDES INDUSTRIAL ROBOTS THAT SWIFTLY HELP CREATE THE COMPANY'S SURFACE-MOUNT INTEGRATED CIRCUIT BOARDS. MANUFACTURING ENGINEER DICENSO ASSISTS AN EMPLOYEE MAKING AN ADJUSTMENT TO A PICK & PLACE MANUFACTURING ROBOT.

INDUSTRIAL & FINANCIAL SYSTEMS' (IFS) BUSINESS CONCEPT IS SIMPLE: TO INCREASE THE FREEDOM OF ACTION AND COMPETITIVE-NESS OF ENTERPRISES BY OFFERING STANDARDIZED BUSINESS SYSTEMS BASED ON LEADING TECHNOLOGIES. "WE'RE MORE OF A solutions company than a software company," says John S. Bridges III, vice president of marketing. "We offer large-business software solutions."

As one of the world's top 10 enterprise resource-planning vendors, IFS uses component-based technology to help businesses meet their needs. The Sweden-based company employs more than 2,000 people around the world, and sales, implementation, and support of IFS Applications are performed through an international organization of wholly and jointly owned companies, as well as through a network of distributors. IFS counts among its customers many Fortune 2,000 companies, including Qualcomm, Caterpillar, Ericsson, and Volvo.

Established in 1983, IFS started its Tucson operations in 1996; the University of Arizona was one of the biggest reasons the company set up shop in Tucson. "It's continued to be a very good source of highly qualified people," says Bridges. "Employees are encouraged to think creatively. They're not cogs. They're a general resource that contributes to the overall good."

The company currently employs some 120 people in Tucson, and recently expanded into its building on Finance Center Drive. In the future, IFS plans to grow its workforce to some 250 employees locally.

IFS APPLICATIONS

IFS Applications is based on technology that offers greater flexibility and freedom of action than other business systems. Through IFS, businesses are able to shape systems to meet specific requirements. IFS Applications allows customers to use new information technology without major upgrading, thereby changing their ways of doing business and helping them to take advantage of new opportunities as they arise.

IFS business management solutions are built on leading information technology. The company offers a breadth of functionality and a proven record of accomplishment with many medium-sized and large companies. Businesses can start small with just the functions they need, working with an existing system or standing alone. As businesses grow and their needs change, more IFS modules allow them to add users, loca-

tions, or functionality. This capability creates an integrated solution that spans all business processes, departments, and units. For international operations, IFS Applications also supports multiple currencies, languages, and sites.

IFS offers a wide range of systems to fit customers' particular needs. The applications are designed using a component-based architecture, and businesses can choose from 40 modules. The modules can be combined to exact specifications and can be chosen, added, or adapted independently of each other.

IFS believes that the time, money, and effort companies put into their new business solutions should produce instant benefits. Therefore, the firm starts with business-critical processes instead of forcing companies into a complete business process reengineering overhaul.

The new solution can quickly become productive because the modules are installed in parallel. A business can put one module into operation the moment it's ready without having to wait for the others. This allows older systems to be replaced over time and at a company's own pace.

▶ JONATHAN POSTAL

INDUSTRIAL & FINANCIAL SYSTEMS (IFS) CURRENTLY EMPLOYS SOME 120 PEOPLE IN TUCSON, AND RECENTLY EXPANDED INTO ITS BUILDING ON FINANCE CENTER DRIVE. IN THE FUTURE, THE COMPANY PLANS TO GROW ITS WORKFORCE TO SOME 250 EMPLOYEES LOCALLY.

As one of the world's top 10 enterprise resource-planning vendors, Sweden-based IFS established its Tucson office in 1996.

IFS uses the best tools on the market, allowing it to leverage to its advantage the dollars that companies such as Microsoft, Oracle, and Rational invest in research and development every year. That also means technical support is available around the world, giving companies greater freedom.

Easy Upgrades

To make upgrades effortless and seamless, the company manages installations with the IFS Active Quality & Distribution System (QDS). This system stores descriptions of a business' specific solution during its entire lifetime. Although it's built with standard components, each installation of IFS Applications is unique, with specific adaptations to industry, business, or customer needs. QDS tracks changes such as when, how, and where hardware and software upgrades are made and which new software modules are implemented. This system allows for easier maintenance.

IFS has also made it easier for workers to define their personal electronic workspaces, allowing them to be tailored to suit a broad range of users. Because all IFS Applications modules have the same look and feel, as well as the same graphical interface found in Windows, users will be up and running in a very short amount of time.

IFS gets companies involved in the implementation process during require-

ments analysis, prototyping, project management, and training. This focus translates into lower costs and faster implementation, as well as wider acceptance of the new system. Thanks to the transfer of knowledge, it also means less dependence on the vendor.

Not only does the company's technology top those of its competitors, IFS also provides long-term support to users

of its software. "We not only sell software, but we understand customers' needs in real life," Bridges says. "We're going to have a long-term relationship with our customers."

IFS' aim is to be a billion-dollar company in the very near future. With a focus on continuing customer service and state-of-the-art technology, the firm is sure to successfully achieve its goal.

The University of Arizona was one of the biggest reasons the company set up shop in Tucson. "It's continued to be a very good source of highly qualified people," says John S. Bridges III, vice president of marketing.

HAMPTON INN NORTH IS A RELATIVE NEWCOMER TO TUCSON'S LODGING SCENE, BUT IT'S ALREADY BECOME ONE OF THE CITY'S MOST SUCCESSFUL HOTELS. OPENED IN 1997, THE FIVE-STORY, 92-ROOM HOTEL NEXT TO INTERSTATE 10 MAINTAINS

a 92 percent retention rate. "Ninety-two percent of the guests who stay here now say they will return," explains General Manager Laurel Preston, who adds that it's due to the hotel's commitment to guest service and its money-back guarantee. "We guarantee high-quality accommodations, friendly and efficient service, and clean, comfortable sur- roundings," says Preston, who's worked in the hospitality industry for 10 years. "If you're not completely satisfied, we don't expect you to pay.

"We pride ourselves on running a friendly staff," adds Preston. "Our front desk is one of the friendliest in town, and the staff is empowered to take care of any problems that may arise."

THE STANDARD OF SUCCESS

Hampton Inn is just three miles from downtown Tucson, the University of Arizona, and Tucson Mall. It's also 10 miles from Old Tucson Studios, the Arizona-Sonora Desert Museum, and

Tucson National Golf Course. "Most of our business comes right off the free- way. We want guests to feel welcome from the minute they walk in the door," says Preston.

Rooms feature a unique south- western design, microwave ovens, refrigerators, free local phone calls, and 25-inch, remote-control TVs with cable and HBO. Guests can choose from many room types, including kings, double queens, king studies, and deluxe whirlpool suites. Seventy-five percent of the rooms are designated nonsmok- ing. The hotel also features a hospitality suite for meetings or social gatherings; a heated, outdoor pool and spa; valet laundry service; and a complimentary breakfast bar.

"Hampton Inn has a very strict standard as to what we have in our rooms, and what we look like," Preston adds. "The number one reason a guest stays at the hotel is cleanliness." So, Hampton Inn strives to provide such an atmosphere for all of its guests. In addition, Hampton Inn was the first

chain hotel to offer a 100 percent guest satisfaction guarantee.

Preston is enjoying success in her first assignment as general manager of a property. Despite a very competitive market in Tucson, Hampton Inn is draw- ing its share of guests who appreciate comfort, service, and surroundings. Guests who completed recent surveys on quality assurance ranked Hampton Inn very highly. On a recent Quality Insurance inspection conducted by the Hampton Inn Corporation, the Hampton Inn North received an outstanding rating. Guests rated the hotel on categories such as overall product, overall service, and problem resolution.

EXPERIENCED MANAGEMENT

The hotel is owned by Zenith Man- agement Co., which has a national reputation as a developer of new hotels in strategic locations, as well as for being turn-around experts for older properties. Zenith has more than 50 years' experience in real estate and

HAMPTON INN NORTH IN TUCSON IS ONE OF THE CITY'S MOST SUCCESSFUL HOTELS.

retail and more than 30 years' experience in lodging operations.

Zenith follows a three-part formula. The company enhances values through creating new buildings and additions, remodeling, upgrading, and refranchising. Zenith also controls expenses with meaningful budgets, efficient management, and careful scrutiny of operating expenses to reduce costs. Finally, it boosts sales through dynamic advertising and multifaceted sales promotions.

The company's expertise was particularly apparent during the 1990-1993 recession, when Zenith-managed properties averaged 69 percent occupancy rates, 6 percent higher than the industry average. Zenith bought its first hotel in 1967 in Duluth, Minnesota, the company's home base. Currently, the company totals 2,980 rooms and 29 properties around the country. In addition to the two properties in Tucson, Zenith features eight other hotels in Arizona, including a Hampton Inn in Peoria, six properties in Scottsdale, and a Holiday Inn in Lake Havasu City. Before Zenith expands into new markets, the company carefully researches an area to ensure there's a high consumer demand for rooms.

Zenith also owns the 147-room Rodeway Inn across the street from the Hampton Inn in Tucson. That property was bought in 1992 and completely renovated. The company added a permanent, 16,800-foot exhibition hall to the Rodeway Inn in 1996. The hall and an additional 280-foot tent are occupied twice a year by Gem & Lapidary Wholesalers, Inc. as part of Tucson's world-renowned international gem show.

For the future, Preston says, the Hampton Inn will maintain its commitment to a high standard of guest service and clean, comfortable, well-appointed guest rooms. And that commitment will ensure that Hampton Inn North, one of Tucson's newest hotels, will also be one of its most successful hotels for many years to come.

HIGH QUALITY. FAMILY FRIENDLY. COMMUNITY ORIENTED. THESE KEY PHRASES SUM UP THE PROGRAMMING OF KWBA-TV58. "THESE SIMPLE BUT IMPORTANT IDEAS REPRESENT THE BEST WAYS TO ATTRACT AND KEEP AUDIENCES," SAYS EXECUTIVE

Vice President and General Manager Ron Bergamo. "If you promote a station right, you'll win the hearts and minds of the viewers."

When KWBA-TV burst onto the scene on New Year's Eve 1998, the southern Arizona region hadn't had a new TV station since the 1980s. It was also one of the largest markets left in the country that wasn't served by the WB Network. Today, thanks to its 5 million-watt signal broadcast from the Santa Rita Mountains south of Tucson, KWBA-TV is seen throughout southern Arizona from Marana to Mexico. It can also be seen on cable channel 8.

The mission of KWBA-TV is to serve the entire southern Arizona region by offering the highest-quality entertainment programming and through meaningful community involvement. By focusing on community and viewer needs, the station hopes to truly become Southern Arizona's Own—while hopefully becoming one of the region's most popular and most watched television stations.

A STATION THAT CARES

KWBA stands out as a community station that cares. One of the station's community-oriented features is *Southern Arizona Prime*, a series of short profiles on upbeat happenings around the region. Airing throughout the day, the stories are KWBA-TV's window on the people, places, and events of southern Arizona.

The wide-ranging feature focuses on a variety of subject matter from all over the region.

At the heart of *Southern Arizona Prime* are the stories that reflect the diverse heritage and rich history of the area. The segments draw on a range of resources, including community leaders, area schools, and nonprofit organizations. Segment topics have included the Special Olympics, a teen town hall, and the restoration of Kentucky Camp, a turn-of-the-century mining camp south of Tucson. "There's no agenda, just good stories,"

says Bergamo. "A lot of good things are happening."

THAT'S ENTERTAINMENT

The station also has a wide range of entertainment offerings, from classic episodes of *I Love Lucy* to the more modern *7th Heaven*, the WB Network's top-rated show. Prime-time offerings include the shows that everyone is talking about: *Dawson's Creek*, *Felicity*, *Charmed*, and *Buffy the Vampire Slayer*.

Late at night and late in the afternoon, KWBA-TV features funny favorites

THE MISSION OF KWBA-TV58 IS TO SERVE THE ENTIRE SOUTHERN ARIZONA REGION BY OFFERING THE HIGHEST-QUALITY ENTERTAINMENT PROGRAMMING, SUCH AS *DAWSON'S CREEK* (BOTTOM RIGHT) AND *FRIENDS* (TOP RIGHT).

THROUGH ITS CONTINUING COMMUNITY INVOLVEMENT AND ITS FOCUS ON MEETING VIEWER'S NEEDS, KWBA-TV58 HAS QUICKLY ACCOMPLISHED ITS MISSION OF BECOMING AN IMPORTANT PART OF THE REGION. THE STATION IS TRULY SOUTHERN ARIZONA'S OWN, WITH FAMILY-FRIENDLY PROGRAMMING AND A SPACIOUS LOBBY THAT WELCOMES VIEWERS TO THE FACILITY (BOTTOM LEFT).

like *Friends*, *Cheers*, *Roseanne*, *Grace Under Fire,* and *The Fresh Prince of Bel-Air*. Kids are treated to an all-star lineup from the leader in children's animation—Warner Bros. Shows include *Pokémon*, *Batman*, *Superman*, *Pinky and the Brain*, *Animaniacs*, and *Histeria!*, a show about history for kids that is narrated by kids.

Viewers can watch all the action of the Arizona Diamondbacks when they catch the games on KWBA-TV. In addition, the station covers Arizona Cardinals preseason events, as well as University of Arizona football and basketball, and provides the latest updates on national sports.

Every Saturday night, the stars shine bright on KWBA-TV in some of Hollywood's finest films. Viewers can also check out movies Saturday and Sunday afternoon. In addition, daytime dramas like *Matlock* and *Hawaii Five-O* keep viewers on the edges of their seats, matching wits with television's top sleuths. They can also check out what's happening outside with weather updates put together by the station's state-of-the-art equipment. The detailed weather forecasts give the whole picture and inform the viewer of any weather changes, airing on the hour from 4 to 10 p.m.

The variety of programming offered by KWBA-TV means the station attracts advertising from across the spectrum, not just ad campaigns aimed specifically at children or seniors. "You may not like *Pokémon* or the Diamondbacks, but you might like an old episode of *The Andy Griffith Show*," explains Bergamo. "Since four out of 10 people don't have cable, you have to have a good signal and good programming."

KWBA-TV's goal is to reach as many people as possible in the area. By concentrating on quality programming that appeals to a diverse audience, the station now reaches 10 to 12 percent more households than other stations in the region. Through its continuing community involvement and its focus on meeting the viewer's needs, KWBA-TV has quickly accomplished its mission of becoming an important part of the southern Arizona region.

FROM LOCALLY THEMED ARIZONA AVENUE TO THE NATION'S BIGGEST DEPARTMENT STORE CHAINS, THE TUCSON MALL OFFERS GOODS FOR SHOPPERS OF EVERY STRIPE. TWO HUNDRED STORES EMPLOYING MORE THAN 2,000 PEOPLE OFFER PRODUCTS AND

services ranging from bath gel to sandals to manicures to diamond rings.

With its wealth of retailers offering high-quality clothing and accessories, the mall brings to Tucson a diversity of highly selective, high-end shops, such as Banana Republic, Guess?, and Old Navy, as well as national department stores and locally owned shops. "The tenants are our number one strength," says Rocco A. Miller, general manager.

Providing the community the best and most comfortable shopping environment possible is a goal the retail facility has continued to strive for since its opening in 1982. "The challenge is trying to stay ahead of everyone," Miller says. "We would like to think we mirror Tucson in what we do and what we offer."

MAKING FAMILIES WELCOME
The Tucson Mall expanded in 1991, adding 40 more shops and the Robinsons-May department store to serve the city's rapidly growing population. The mall also redesigned its food court in 1993 and added a colorful carousel. "We

thought it would be attractive to the families and extend their stay," Miller says.

In addition, children can participate in the mall's Kidz Club, an entertainment program held on the first and third Tuesday of each month. More than 100 kids attend the monthly events, which include musical, dance, and puppet shows. Meanwhile, parents can take advantage of Hot Nights, Cool Jazz. Held in June and July, the popular program offers live jazz from 6 to 8 p.m.

Arizona Avenue grew out of the food court renovation. The stretch of Southwest-themed gift shops, which sell items like salsa, jewelry, and T-shirts, was installed at the end of 1993, taking over an area once occupied by food vendors. It is now one of the most successful and unique parts of the mall.

The Tucson Mall has also added restaurants like 5 & Diner and Marie Callender's to the property on its periphery. "If you make your mall the hub where you have everything," Miller says, "people are going to go there."

LOOKING TO THE FUTURE
Owned by Cleveland-based Forest City Enterprises, Tucson Mall belongs to one of the top 25 mall developers in the country. Forest City is working hard to further improve the facility, and that financial commitment is paying off. "We average $425 per square foot in sales. That's a huge number," Miller says, adding that $300 per square foot is average for most malls.

The mall's marketing staff works to publicize the retail center around southern Arizona and in Mexico, and to make the center accessible to shoppers throughout the area. For example, shuttle buses bring in visitors from downtown, area resorts, and the airport. Shuttle traffic also helps the mall keep track of its peak seasons.

In the future, the Tucson Mall plans to add more clothing and fashion stores, and is also pursuing a cinema deal. Further renovations are also in the works to ensure that Tucson Mall remains on the forefront of shopping pleasure.

CLOCKWISE FROM BOTTOM LEFT: WITH ITS BRIGHT AND AIRY SETTING, WIDE SELECTION OF SHOPS AND SERVICES, AND EXCITING MARKETING EVENTS AND PROMOTIONS, THE TUCSON MALL IS ONE OF SOUTHERN ARIZONA'S FAVORITE PLACES TO SHOP.

THE TUCSON MALL FEATURES A UNIQUE CORRIDOR OF LOCAL SOUTHWESTERN SHOPS, CALLED ARIZONA AVENUE. SHOPPERS CAN FIND AUTHENTIC REGIONAL SPICES AND CERAMICS, AS WELL AS BEAUTIFUL JEWELRY AND APPAREL, IN THIS STRETCH OF SHOPS.

THE TUCSON MALL IS A 1.3 MILLION-SQUARE-FOOT REGIONAL SHOPPING CENTER OFFERING MORE THAN 200 SPECIALTY SHOPS, MORE THAN 20 FOOD VENDORS AND RESTAURANTS, AND SIX MAJOR DEPARTMENT STORES, INCLUDING DILLARD'S, JCPENNEY, MACY'S, MERVYN'S, ROBINSONS-MAY, AND SEARS.

BEGINNING AS A SMALL PUBLISHER OF LOCAL NEWSPAPERS IN THE 1930S, TOWERY PUBLISHING, INC. TODAY PRODUCES A WIDE RANGE OF COMMUNITY-ORIENTED MATERIALS, INCLUDING BOOKS (URBAN TAPESTRY SERIES), BUSINESS DIRECTORIES,

magazines, and Internet publications. Building on its long heritage of excellence, the company has become global in scope, with cities from San Diego to Sydney represented by Towery products. In all its endeavors, this Memphis-based company strives to be synonymous with service, utility, and quality.

A DIVERSITY OF COMMUNITY-BASED PRODUCTS

Over the years, Towery has become the largest producer of published materials for North American chambers of commerce. From membership directories that enhance business-to-business communication to visitor and relocation guides tailored to reflect the unique qualities of the communities they cover, the company's chamber-oriented materials offer comprehensive information on

dozens of topics, including housing, education, leisure activities, health care, and local government.

In 1998, the company acquired Cincinnati-based Target Marketing, an established provider of detailed city street maps to more than 300 chambers of commerce throughout the United States and Canada. Now a division of Towery, Target offers full-color maps that include local landmarks and points of interest, such as parks, shopping centers, golf courses, schools, industrial parks, city and county limits, subdivision names, public buildings, and even block numbers on most streets.

In 1990, Towery launched the Urban Tapestry Series, an award-winning collection of oversized, hardbound photojournals detailing the people, history, culture, environment, and commerce of various metropolitan areas. These coffee-table

books highlight a community through three basic elements: an introductory essay by a noted local individual, an exquisite collection of four-color photographs, and profiles of the companies and organizations that animate the area's business life.

To date, more than 80 Urban Tapestry Series editions have been published in cities around the world, from New York to Vancouver to Sydney. Authors of the books' introductory essays include former U.S. President Gerald Ford (Grand Rapids), former Alberta Premier Peter Lougheed (Calgary), CBS anchor Dan Rather (Austin), ABC anchor Hugh Downs (Phoenix), best-selling mystery author Robert B. Parker (Boston), American Movie Classics host Nick Clooney (Cincinnati), Senator Richard Lugar (Indianapolis), and Challenger Center founder June Scobee Rodgers (Chattanooga).

To maintain hands-on quality in all of its periodicals and books, Towery has long used the latest production methods available. The company was the first production environment in the United States to combine desktop publishing with color separations and image scanning to produce finished film suitable for burning plates for four-color printing. Today, Towery relies on state-of-the-art digital prepress services to produce more than 8,000 pages each year, containing more than 30,000 high-quality color images.

AN INTERNET PIONEER

By combining its long-standing expertise in community-oriented published materials with advanced production capabilities, a global sales force, and extensive data management expertise, Towery has emerged as a significant provider of Internet-based city information. In keeping with its overall focus on community resources, the company's Internet efforts represent a natural step in the evolution of the business.

The primary product lines within the Internet division are the introCity™ sites. Towery's introCity sites introduce newcomers, visitors, and longtime residents to every facet of a particular community, while simultaneously placing the

TOWERY PUBLISHING, INC. PRESIDENT AND CEO J. ROBERT TOWERY HAS EXPANDED THE BUSINESS HIS PARENTS STARTED IN THE 1930S TO INCLUDE A GROWING ARRAY OF TRADITIONAL AND ELECTRONIC PUBLISHED MATERIALS, AS WELL AS INTERNET AND MULTIMEDIA SERVICES, THAT ARE MARKETED LOCALLY, NATIONALLY, AND INTERNATIONALLY.

local chamber of commerce at the fore-front of the city's Internet activity. The sites include newcomer information, calendars, photos, citywide business listings with everything from nightlife to shopping to family fun, and on-line maps pinpointing the exact location of businesses, schools, attractions, and much more.

DECADES OF PUBLISHING EXPERTISE

In 1972, current President and CEO J. Robert Towery succeeded his parents in managing the printing and publishing business they had founded nearly four decades earlier. Soon thereafter, he expanded the scope of the company's published materials to include *Memphis* magazine and other successful regional and national publications. In 1985, after selling its locally focused assets, Towery began the trajectory on which it contin-ues today, creating community-oriented materials that are often produced in con-junction with chambers of commerce and other business organizations.

Despite the decades of change, Towery himself follows a long-standing family philosophy of unmatched service and unflinching quality. That approach extends throughout the entire organiza-tion to include more than 130 employees at the Memphis headquarters, another

60 located in Northern Kentucky outside Cincinnati, and more than 50 sales, marketing, and editorial staff traveling to and working in a growing list of client cities. All of its products, and more infor-mation about the company, are featured on the Internet at www.towery.com.

In summing up his company's steady growth, Towery restates the essen-

tial formula that has driven the business since its first pages were published: "The creative energies of our staff drive us toward innovation and invention. Our people make the highest possible de-mands on themselves, so I know that our future is secure if the ingredients for success remain a focus on service and quality."

TOWERY PUBLISHING WAS THE FIRST PRODUCTION ENVIRONMENT IN THE UNITED STATES TO COMBINE DESKTOP PUBLISHING WITH COLOR SEPARATIONS AND IMAGE SCANNING TO PRODUCE FINISHED FILM SUITABLE FOR BURNING PLATES FOR FOUR-COLOR PRINTING. TODAY, THE COMPANY'S STATE-OF-THE-ART NETWORK OF MACINTOSH AND WINDOWS WORKSTATIONS ALLOWS IT TO PRODUCE MORE THAN 8,000 PAGES EACH YEAR, CONTAINING MORE THAN 30,000 HIGH-QUALITY COLOR IMAGES.

THE TOWERY FAMILY'S PUBLISHING ROOTS CAN BE TRACED TO 1935, WHEN R.W. TOWERY (FAR LEFT) BEGAN PRODUCING A SERIES OF COMMUNITY HISTORIES IN TENNESSEE, MISSISSIPPI, AND TEXAS. THROUGHOUT THE COM-PANY'S HISTORY, THE FOUNDING FAM-ILY HAS CONSISTENTLY EXHIBITED A COMMITMENT TO CLARITY, PRECISION, INNOVATION, AND VISION.

PHOTOGRAPHERS

Allsport was founded the moment freelance photographer Tony Duffy captured the now-famous picture of Bob Beamon breaking the world long-jump record at the Mexico City Olympics in 1968. Originally head-quartered in London, Allsport has expanded to include offices in New York and Los Angeles. Its pictures have appeared in every major publication in the world, and the best of its portfolio has been displayed at elite photographic exhibitions at the Royal Photographic Society and the Olympic Museum in Lausanne.

Originally from New York, **Gary Auerbach** is vice president of Triple A Pistachios. He specializes in platinum printmaking of portraits and cityscapes, and his work can be viewed on-line at www.azstarnet.com/platinum.

Alan Benoit received a bachelor of fine arts degree from Arizona State University. His photographs have appeared in numerous publications, including *Travel & Leisure*, *Condé Nast Traveler*, *USA Today*, *Arizona Highways*, and *National Geographic Traveler*, as well as in Towery Publishing's *Greater Phoenix: The Desert in Bloom*. Benoit is a four-time winner of the Nikon/Outdoor Writers of America's *Great American Outdoors* exhibition.

Brett Drury owns and operates Brett Drury Architectural Photography. His clients include leading architecture, interior design, and contracting firms in Tucson and throughout the West.

José Galvez was a member of the *Los Angeles Times* reporting team that won a 1984 Pulitzer Prize in public service for an in-depth examination of southern California's growing Latino community. A native of Tucson, he has published several books, and his work has been exhibited throughout the United States and Mexico.

Heather Gravning enjoys photograph-ing plants, animals, and landscapes. Her specialty, however, is capturing lightning on film, and Tucson's infamous monsoon season provides more than adequate inspiration.

Originally from Sacramento, California, **Bruce Griffin** has called Tucson home since 1974. Owner of Bruce Griffin Scenic Nature Photography, he specializes in images of the Sonoran Desert. Griffin's work has appeared in *Arizona Highways*, as well as in numerous calendars.

Stacey Halper received a bachelor of fine arts degree in photography from the State University of New York (SUNY)-Purchase College. Her work has been exhibited in galleries in New York, Connecticut, and Arizona, as well as appearing in Towery Publishing's *New York: A State of Mind*, and she recently participated in a group show at the Kodak Gallery in Seoul. Halper is also in the process of finishing her first short film, *Bread and Bones*.

Gregory Harris is employed by Bombardier Aerospace. He has traveled to all of the lower 48 states, as well as to six Canadian provinces. In his scenic photography, Harris strives to "evoke both the awe of nature, and the nature of awe."

As owner of Totally Tucson, **Fred Hood** specializes in photographs of wild animals and desert scenes. A native of California, he received a bachelor of arts degree in religious studies from California State University and a master of divinity degree from Fuller Theological Seminary.

Darin Ipema, originally from Chicago, received a bachelor of fine arts degree in communication from the University of Memphis. He specializes in cinema-tography, and has shot two independent feature films, as well as several music videos. Ipema's photographs have also appeared in Towery Publishing's *Greater Phoenix: The Desert in Bloom*, *New York: A State of Mind*, and *St. Louis: For the Record*.

Gill Kenny has won more than 300 state, regional, national, and interna-tional awards for design, art direction,

and photography. He specializes in corporate, industrial, and travel images, and enjoys photographing rock climbing, scuba diving, and sailing.

James Lemass studied art in his native Ireland before moving to Cambridge, Massachusetts, in 1987. His areas of specialty include people and travel photography, and his work can be seen in publications by Aer Lingus, British Airways, and USAir, as well as the Nynex Yellow Pages. Lemass has also worked for the Massachusetts Office of Travel and Tourism, and his photo-graphs have appeared in several other Towery publications, including *Greater Phoenix: The Desert in Bloom*; *New York: Metropolis of the American Dream*; *Northern Kentucky: Looking to the New Millennium*; *Orlando: The City Beautiful*; *San Diego: World-Class City*; *Treasures on Tampa Bay: Tampa, St. Petersburg, Clearwater*; and *Washington: City on a Hill*.

A native of Indiana, **William Lesch** moved to the Tucson area in 1973. His photographs have appeared in galleries from Baltimore to Madrid. Lesch has also received numerous grants and awards from organizations including the Tempe Arts Commission, the Scottsdale Center for the Arts, and the Arizona Commission on the Arts.

Edward McCain's clients include *Arizona Highways*, *Sunset Magazine*, and Samsung Telecommunications. He received a bachelor of journalism degree from the University of Missouri-Columbia.

Debs Metzong served in the U.S. Army, where he did some military photography while stationed in Japan. He was employed by Mountain Bell/US West for 32 years, including 10 years as a photographer, until his retirement. Metzong now freelances regularly, and his photographs also have appeared in Towery Publishing's *Greater Phoenix: The Desert in Bloom*.

Chris Mooney is employed by Balfour Walker Studios, and he specializes in sports, people, and stock photography. He currently photographs rugby around the world for Lands' End, Inc.

Erwin "Bud" Nielsen, a certified professional photographer and New York School of Photography graduate, is the proprietor of Tucson-based Images International studio. With a collection of more than 100,000 stock images, Nielsen offers pictures of geographical locations throughout the United States, Europe, Africa, the Far East, and Central and South America. Subjects range from nature and people to travel and tourism. His clients include a plethora of magazines, newspapers, calendar and card companies, travel-industry businesses, book publishers, and advertising agencies, and his photographs have appeared in Towery Publishing's *San Antonio: A Cultural Tapestry*. In addition to having a permanent gallery in Phoenix—the Finch Gallery—Nielsen is also represented by stock agencies located in California, New Hampshire, New Jersey, Australia, Belgium, and Germany.

Laurence Parent received a bachelor of science degree in petroleum engineering from the University of Texas. Owner of Laurence Parent Photography, he has contributed photographs to *Texas Monthly*, *National Geographic*, *Newsweek*, the *New York Times*, *Outside*, and *Texas Highways*, as well as to Towery Publishing's *Austin: Celebrating the Lone Star Millennium*. Parent has published 21 books, and his images have appeared in numerous calendars.

A native of Tucson, **Mary Peachin** is a photojournalist, lecturer, and consultant on adventure travel. In addition to her electronic publication, www.peachin.com, she freelances for both newspapers and magazines. Peachin is a member of the Society of American Travel Writers and her photography is represented by Photo 20-20 in San Francisco.

Photophile, established in San Diego in 1967, is owned and operated by Nancy Likins-Masten. An internationally known stock photography agency, the company houses more than a million color images, and represents more than 90 contributing local and international photographers. Subjects include extensive coverage of the West Coast, business/industry, people/lifestyles, health/medicine, travel, scenics, wildlife, and adventure sports, plus 200 additional categories.

James Randklev is a 24-year veteran travel and scenic photographer. His clients include *Omni*, *Travel & Leisure*, Anheuser-Busch, American Express, *National Geographic Explorer*, and Nike. Randklev is one of the Sierra Club's most published calendar photographers.

James P. Rowan owns and operates the Chicago-based James P. Rowan Photography. He has amassed a clientele that includes textbooks, children's books, and magazines. Rowan annually adds thousands of images to his stock file, which currently holds approximately 300,000 images.

Bob Willis, a former television travel host, is a self-taught photographer. A member of the Society of American Travel Writers, he is a travel guidebook writer for Fodor's, Access Guides, and Globe Pequot Press. Willis is a two-time top winner of the Chesapeake Bay Photo Contest, and his images have been used by Teldon Calendars and on a U.S. Commerce Department poster, as well as in Towery Publishing's *Greater Phoenix: The Desert in Bloom*.

Additional photographers and organizations that contributed to *Tucson: High Desert Harmony* include the Arizona Historical Society, David Elms, GeoIMAGERY, International Stock, Michael Stack, and Lynn Taber.

Towery Publishing, Inc.
The Towery Building, 1835 Union Avenue, Memphis, TN 38104
www.towery.com

■ PUBLISHER: J. Robert Towery ■ EXECUTIVE PUBLISHER: Jenny McDowell ■ NATIONAL SALES MANAGER: Stephen Hung ■ MARKETING DIRECTOR: Carol Culpepper ■ PROJECT DIRECTORS: Carolyn Cortez, Robert Delmar, Andrea Glazier, Carol Hildebrandt

■ EXECUTIVE EDITOR: David B. Dawson ■ MANAGING EDITOR: Lynn Conlee ■ SENIOR EDITOR: Carlisle Hacker ■ EDITOR/PROFILE MANAGER: Stephen M. Deusner ■ EDITORS: Jana Files, Brian Johnston, Ginny Reeves, Sunni Thompson ■ ASSISTANT EDITOR: Rebecca Green ■ EDITORIAL ASSISTANT: Emily Haire ■ PROFILE WRITER: Katherine Drouin Keith ■ CAPTION WRITER: Scott Barker

■ CREATIVE DIRECTOR: Brian Groppe ■ PHOTOGRAPHY EDITOR: Jonathan Postal ■ PROFILE DESIGNERS: Laurie Beck, Melissa Ellis, Ann Ward ■ PRODUCTION MANAGER: Brenda Pattat ■ PHOTOGRAPHY COORDINATOR: Robin Lankford ■ PRODUCTION ASSISTANT: Loretta Drew ■ DIGITAL COLOR SUPERVISOR: Darin Ipema ■ DIGITAL COLOR TECHNICIANS: Eric Friedl, Deidre Kesler, Brent Salazar, Mark Svetz ■ PRODUCTION RESOURCES MANAGER: Dave Dunlap Jr. ■ PRINT COORDINATOR: Beverly Timmons

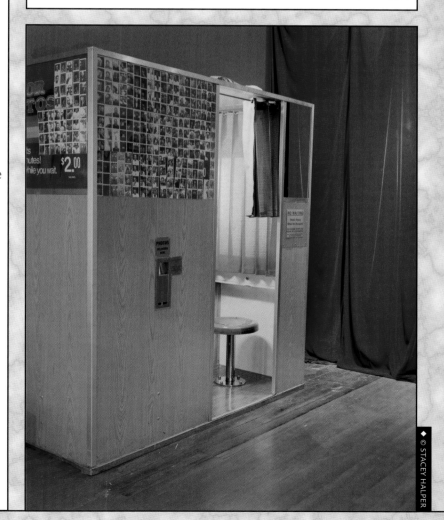

© STACEY HALPER

INDEX OF PROFILES

Library of Congress Cataloging-in-Publication Data

Tucson : high desert harmony / by the Ronstadt Family ; art direction by Geoffrey Ellis.
     p. cm. — (Urban tapestry series)
Includes index.
ISBN 1-881096-77-7 (alk. paper)
 1. Tucson (Ariz.)—Civilization. 2. Tucson (Ariz.)—Pictorial works. 3. Tucson
(Ariz.)—Economic conditions. 4. Business enterprises—Arizona—Tucson. I. Series.

F819.T95 T83 2000
979.1'776—dc21   99-086983